KIRSTEN BEVERLEY-WATERS

STRUGGLE
GURU

THE BIOGRAPHICAL STRUGGLES THAT
ARE INFLUENCING OUR BIOLOGY

Aiiro Wellness
info@aiirowellness.com
Portland, ME
www.aiirowellness.com

Printed in the United States of America

BookBaby Publishing
7905 N Crescent Blvd
Pennsauken, NJ 08110

ISBN: 978-1-09831-254-1

First Edition, 2020

I DEDICATE THIS BOOK to every person that ever saw struggle as a weakness. May your struggles be set free to share their lessons and stories, and awaken the guru within you.

CONTENTS

ACKNOWLEDGMENTS

WRITING A BOOK IS HARDER THAN I THOUGHT, AND MORE REWARD-
ing than I could have ever imagined.

None of this would have been possible without the support and love of my dear wife Korrie. She constantly reminds me of the power of one human being believing in you. Through her belief and encouragement, I found my voice and the courage to use it to help others. *Words will never fully express the ways in which my life has been forever changed by your partnership.*

I'm eternally grateful to my mother, Teri Beverley. I first learned what it meant to overcome struggle through her exam-ple. She taught me discipline, tough love, manners, respect, and so much more, all of which has helped me succeed in life. No words could possibly express the extent of my love and grati-tude for all of her sacrifice. *Thank you for never giving up on me and my journey.*

To my sisters, Constance and Kendra, opposites in their ways of living life but united in their power to be examples of perseverance and hard work: *I am so proud to call both of you my sisters.*

To my yoga teachers Tiffany Cruikshank, Kathryn Budig, Almut Schotte, Alice Louise, Valerie Knopik, and Tracy Rhinehart: *The practices you shared on the mat transcended the asana and transformed the way I see practice as a way of teaching and living.*

To my pastor Michael, who shook the tree of knowledge in my heart and helped me sort through the many questions of faith: *Your guidance will always be a light on my path.*

To the many friends and teachers who have poured into my life and helped me navigate the ways of this world: *There are too many of you to mention by name, but each of you holds a special place in my heart.*

Lastly, thank you to my father, who will never read these words, but whose brief life on earth still lives through me.

INVITATION

*"One day, in retrospect, the years of struggle will
strike you as the most beautiful."*

—SIGMUND FREUD

DEAR STRUGGLE GURU,

It's long overdue that we meet the guru...

The tattoos of struggle painted across your body make me
certain you are the one that I have been seeking. If it makes you
a bit uneasy to know that I see your struggle from a distance,
you are not alone: Struggles feel like gaping wounds and scars
that have mutilated our bodies, and the idea that they could
be seen as pieces of art that uniquely share a personal journey
seems possible only in the literary. Let me reassure you: *You may
not see the wisdom in your achievements and falters in struggle, but I do.*

Here, in these pages, we will explore together, unravelling the
teachings of your struggles that are locked within you. Together,
we will sort through the mess that makes each of us our greatest
student and teacher. The years of struggling that have felt like a
dark cloud on your purpose and potential will be lifted.

It's time to see the years of struggle as the most beautiful practices of knowing—your deepest self.

This is **your** moment, guru. Yes, **YOU** are the guru. Perhaps you thought that this book would be the musings of my self-appointed "guruness," but no; it is very much the lessons all of us share in struggle. *Struggle Guru* strips back the labels and layers that separate us.

Here you will crack struggle wide open and see that *every person struggles in life, regardless of where they come from*. It isn't about social class, education, sexual orientation, gender, or religion. The truth is, we all struggle.

Struggle unites us. There are commonalities, and the many curious ways in which struggle unites us and nurtures our growth form the cornerstone of this book.

PRESENT AND HONEST

The only prerequisite this book has is your presence. Struggle, on the other hand, requires a little more than the book: It requires your presence *and* your honesty. If you try to fool struggle, it hits back with more.

Too often, we don't focus on the struggle. Living our day-to-day lives makes it so easy to be distracted, and to try and brush off struggle. Today is not that day. Today, release your trepidation over focusing on your struggles and what you might see. Let go of the fallacy that the turbulent waters are a direct reflection of your true self. Recognize that anything can become distorted if reflected through changing, unruly tides. These watery struggles are not meant to reflect who you are, but to engage you in the navigational journey towards your deeper understanding.

Flip through the pages of this book; wander through these chapters with an explorer's mindset. You don't need to go any deeper than you want (although that also means you cannot blame anyone if your growth becomes limited). From the questions that arise as you read, seek the answers **within**: *You are, after all, the only guru who can truly know your struggle.*

Fear not; it won't all be deep, thought-provoking work. Some lessons rally you through laughter. Others may make you cry. Still others entice you with their promise. *With each and every chapter, there is a good chance a spark will light within you—and fire may begin to blaze.*

If you are ready to explore the Struggle Guru within you, let's dive in together.

Chapter 1

MEET YOUR GURU

*I remember my first visit with my guru. He had shown me that
he could read my mind. So I looked at the grass and thought,
'My God, he's going to know all the things I don't want people to
know.' I was really embarrassed. Then I looked up
and he was looking directly at me with unconditional love.*

—RAM DASS

UNCONDITIONAL LOVE IS CONCEPTUALLY CHALLENGING FOR US TO
extend to ourselves. We judge and measure our choices against
standards that we have been conditioned to believe are the
"right" ones. I have sought many gurus in hopes that their wisdom may unlock some understanding of myself that I turned
a blind eye to, or couldn't connect with, out of my shame or
feeling of unworthiness.

American spiritual teacher Ram Dass speaks to a particularly eye-opening understanding of "guru" that has changed the way in which I understand its meaning. In the epigraph that starts this chapter, notice that he recalls meeting a guru who could read his thoughts, and he experiences shame and fear in this vulnerability. Dass is worried about what others will know, and how that will shape their view of him.

After sitting with this passage for some time, I realized that Dass could very much be speaking to his true self, or his divine inner guru—or that which some might call his consciousness. But let's explore what *you* think about it.

How does this quote change, in knowing this information? (Pause with that for a moment.)

What if he is truly fearful of fully knowing himself, and his deepest thoughts and fears?

To what reality will he be held accountable?

TRUTH KEEPER

As someone who has been teaching for more than a decade, I have watched my students squirm more over fully knowing themselves than sharing their deepest truths with someone whom they hold in high regard. You might argue that this isn't true, but it's the weight of being the only one who knows your truth that crushes you most. It's not the knowing. It's knowing—*and then being known as the only keeper of this truth.*

When the Ram Dass quote continues, you see that the guru looks back with unconditional love. We don't find references to unconditional love in just this quote or context. The acts of unconditional love are referenced in every theology, ideology, and literary story around us.

So how is it that here is where I find myself stuck the most? I might be able to fully dive into the depths of all that I am, both the good and the bad. But to look upon that which is labeled by an external society as "bad" with unconditional love is hardly as simple as uttering the words, "I love myself unconditionally."

To heal through my struggles, I had to venture through the path of unconditional love for myself. I had to let go of the labels and attachments to the "others" in the self-judgments I had created, and release myself of the chains tied to unspoken perfection.

MERCY

Struggle cannot be avoided. It cannot be bought off, or persuaded to come at a more convenient time. I've discovered I can sweep it under the rug and ignore it for a time, but it will only compound in interest, and arise bigger and more overwhelmingly than before.

So why don't I just deal with the struggle when it is in its infancy, instead of waiting until it is built like Dwayne "the Rock" Johnson? Is it that I am a procrastinator at heart? Or do I have some deep-seated belief that I am meant to stay live in the struggle? I think it's a combination of many factors, but all of them go back to my inability to extend unconditional love to myself—to offer myself grace for the ways in which I will fall short. Instead of lingering in my mistakes, I could offer myself mercy and learn from them to grow. After all, "When you know better, you do better," said Maya Angelou.

The world tries to sell us the ideas, experts, experiences, and education containing "the solution" to struggle. But what if the answer was never theirs to give? What if the journey was rerouted for me? What if I am the "one" in one billion people for whom the answer doesn't apply? What then? And most importantly, *why are there so many damn questions to ask myself, and not nearly enough answers?*

Buckle up, because this truth is gonna get bumpy. I cannot offer you "the solution." Yes, I can offer you the personal anecdotes of my own truths, education, and experiences based on what I have learned throughout my life. Yet true potential resides in **STRUGGLE**. And the only guru in my struggle can be me.

The only guru in your struggle? You. That guru comes about through *unconditional love, compassion, deep exploration, and humble failings*.

TIME

As you move through these pages, you will stumble, falter, and question *your* understanding of struggle. You will long for a quick solution that will alleviate the fight.

Give yourself time to arrive. Land here in the present and let your breath smooth out, your jaw unclench, and your eyes soften. Inhale the problems and let the solutions bubble to the surface as you exhale. Open yourself up to the reality that the answers may come in the form of more questions and struggle. Yes, even *more* struggle.

Know that engaging in struggle doesn't mean you are failing or doing it wrong, so don't seek out mastery in struggle in order to feel invincible. Don't do it to win approval or notoriety either. It isn't an achievement or certification you can add to your resume. Becoming the master of yourself is about seeing, for the first time, all the innermost intricacies that have evolved from your life's experiences with unconditional love.

I know what you are thinking: *This sage-smudging, yoga philosophy is not for me.*

Okay, maybe you are "too tough" for this kind of talk. You see yourself as a science-hypothesis-and-solution kind of individual. You pick yourself up by the bootstraps and push forward when it's hard. Feelings are emotions that your life can't afford you to have. Maybe you are like me, and you can't sleep. You feel restless with your thoughts in a quiet moment, and the weight of success feels crushing. But… you might just be all of these people and none of them at any given moment in your life. There comes a point when science seems to fail us, the bootstraps are so worn and tattered we can't grab hold, and the feelings boil over even if we don't want them to. The guru always sees the true self with the eyes of unconditional love. Even if it is buried under the armored guise of its false self.

I'm not here to change your mind. I'm not going to tell you that reading this book will change your life. Let's put forth some realities instead.

THE MESS

Struggle is messy shit. Its truth most times is painful and involves a long hard look in the mirror. You will read a lot of talk in here about compassion, presence, and power. But there is a decent chance I will write at least one thing that offends you, and I don't do it to be insensitive or unkind. Every message comes from a deep respect for all, but also an even deeper call to *shake the way you think.*

The world doesn't need more followers.

The world doesn't need another me.

The world needs you and every other Struggle Guru to unite.

To awaken the guru in you that has been in such a deep slumber, you have to commit to ending the "blame game." Stop pawning your problems off to someone else, sitting back, and complaining that nothing changes. I know how bad that stings, but you are tough enough to hear this truth:

Struggle is your greatest teacher.

It is because of your struggle that you are your greatest guru.

This book is your space to practice, learn, even push the limits of your struggle. Remember, sometimes finding the best life for yourself requires first traveling through hell's fire.

Chapter 2

FOLLOWING THE STARS

*"It is not in the stars to hold our destiny
but in ourselves."*

—WILLIAM SHAKESPEARE

IT WAS WRITTEN IN THE STARS... AT LEAST, THAT IS WHAT MY HORO- scope once read in the girls' magazine *Young and Modern*.

In the pages of this formally popular glossy, I first learned all about what it meant to be a Leo, and how my future would be bright, filled with countless accolades and accomplishments. Being a lion, it was no surprise that I was a natural-born leader, and my roar wasn't just meant to be heard, but also respected. And that's where my understanding of my life's purpose and direction ended. The glossy magazine page filled my mind with thoughts of fame, stardom, and money. But when I flipped the page over, there wasn't a game plan or map on how to achieve such greatness. Instead, on the back page of my horoscope was an advertisement for … weight loss supplements.

Ohhh! That must be what I need for greatness: a smaller waistline! Now I just need to complete enough chores to earn enough money to buy the supplements. Oh, and I need to convince Mom that they are necessary. Piece of cake: Once she knows this is my destiny, how can she deny me??

The answer is, *with ease*. Mom brought me back down to reality and explained that none of the things the magazine promised I was "destined" for would come easily, and they most certainly wouldn't come in a bottle.

But what could she really know? She is a mom, and moms don't know about the mysteries of the universe. She obviously didn't understand how clear the magazine was about my bright and brilliant future.

Funny thing about futures, though—they are unpredictable. (If you are over the age of two, you have probably figured out that mystery of the universe already.) Sure, there are basic outlines of our potential futures scattered along personal paths, like breadcrumbs left there to bait us into staying the course. But for this gluten-intolerant author, those breadcrumbs turned out to be the poison that led me to the witch's house instead of moving me closer to a lavish life of fame and fortune. Although that's saying that the horoscope on the page of *YM* twenty-five -odd years ago was what I really wanted. For while fame and fortune seemed appealing in my youth, as I grew up, I wanted a deep connection with others, and a deep sense of who I am more than I wanted my name to be recognized or my bank account to end in more than nine zeros.

Although to be clear, I would not oppose a larger bank account, just in case the universe is feeling generous.

JUST WHOSE TRUTH?

It's easy to be lured by the glossy airbrushed photos and exotic backdrops we see in the media all around us. Why wouldn't we start to believe this was the purpose for each of us? At its root, fame is really about being seen and heard. Fortune is another way of expressing a desire for security and certainty in some respects. If a little is good, then boatloads must be the absolute best—right?

So, for a time, I became a lost soul traveling through time and space as a copy of another, unintentionally living someone else's truth. It wasn't entirely my fault; I was taught to "fake it until you make it." The horoscope told me it was my "destiny," so I followed her as long as I could, trying to mirror her life plan. I lost sight of finding my path, voice, and truth because I was swept away by—the tide of destiny.

It wasn't until I took a pause and asked, *Am I living my truth, or that of someone else?* that I realized I was just a watered-down version of countless other hopefuls just like myself. My roar was a tiny kitten purr that blended in with everyone else's. I thought that if I followed others who were successful in the ways the world told me I needed to be, I could avoid the pitfalls, failures, and struggles.

FLICKERING GLIMPSES OF YOUR JOURNEY

Concentrated doses of your true self emerge like flickering lights in a thunderstorm. They are a bit unnerving when you don't know what you are looking at, but once you spend enough time around them, they illuminate your path. You may not have thumbed through a magazine when you first caught a glimpse of what "might be" with your future. There could have been several "flickerings" throughout your life that were guiding you. Most of us just break out a flashlight and candles, and hope for the best when we see this happen. Perhaps the darkness of your struggle lies in the missed lessons of your flickering consciousness.

When was the last time you asked yourself, *Whose path am I taking?* Or has the glossy promise of the stars clouded the sky, barring you from navigating your life? Struggle doesn't bind us to stagnation in our lives; we bind ourselves to it by ignoring the signs. In truth, just seeing the flickering isn't enough. Seeing the stars is one thing; understanding the navigational path of the constellation of your life is something completely different.

Chapter 3

COM-PASS YOU ARE

*"Doing as others told me, I was blind.
Coming when others told me, I was lost.
Then I left everyone, myself as well.
Then I found everyone, myself as well."*

—RUMI

MY SENIOR YEAR IN COLLEGE I WAS TAKING A LEADERSHIP TRAIN-
ing course for my business minor. We were divided into teams
for various tasks. Our instructor believed that the best way to
understand the lessons of leadership was to engage in actual
leadership scenarios. One activity in particular stands out in my
mind. It was a team building exercise around the skill of *orienteering*. If you are unfamiliar with orienteering allow me to give
you a quick explanation. Technically speaking and by definition, it requires navigational skills using a map and compass to
navigate from point to point in a diverse and usually unfamiliar

terrain whilst moving for time. Participants are given a topographical map, which is used to find specific control points. Defined from the perspective of a participant in this challenge, it's a 2-hour survival course in how to see your friends as your greatest enemies, stab yourself repeatedly with low hanging branches, and suppress your unquenchable thirst for ringing a bell of surrender just to be freed from the nightmare. Basically they are the same definitions— right? Perhaps, I should elaborate a little further with my story and let you extract your own conclusion.

Handed a compass and a map, I was told that my team needed to find four controls on our orienteering map in a specific order as fast as we could. The goal was to "punch" all tags and be the first team to finish. It would be easy enough if everyone on the team had the same familiarity with orienteering, maps, and compass reading. But the truth is that everyone had a completely *different* background and amount of experience with each of those things. For some, map reading had ended with Siri telling them when to "turn left." Others, however, had grown up in Cub Scouts or survival clubs where they extensively spent time learning all the ins and outs of map and compass reading.

If my team collectively took all of our knowledge and used it, we could effectively navigate the course, and even potentially complete it the fastest. However, that didn't happen: Everyone began shouting over one another, trying to take control. Everyone was an expert who refused to yield to anyone else. This was Freud's perfect example of ego: *Ego flares its temper and refuses to accept anything except its truth*. Finishing first became the priority, not evaluating skills and strengths.

I won't bore you with the yelling, the name-calling, and the number of times we got lost. I'll jump right to the part where we didn't finish first, and wanted to be as far away from one another as possible. We didn't learn anything that day, except that even your closest friends can become your enemy when you are trying to reach success.

I wonder how the story would have played out if we had taken five minutes to evaluate our skills as a team, and then delegate tasks based on our strengths. Actually, though, I don't have to wonder, because my friend Ashley's team did just that—and they won.

Just like this scenario, part of your task as a Struggle Guru is to be able to evaluate your strengths and areas of opportunity. An area of opportunity is a strength *potential*, and not yet a strength, because it needs more time to develop.

As you begin to evaluate yourself, focusing on those priorities that are in the *areas needing the most attention* can create a shift that can take you further from deeper struggle and help you progress. However, in order to evaluate yourself, you need a strong course in personal compass reading. This part might hurt a little: *Your compass is likely broken.* It could be the needle, or an inadvertent set miscalculation of your north. Either way, you are lost.

FOLLOWING BLINDLY

The Sufi mystic and poet Rumi teaches us that when we do as others say, we become blind, and when we come when others call, we become lost (see the epigraph that starts this chapter). The philosophical Rubik's Cube actually says that spending too much time listening to others and following individuals who have what we desire leaves us without skill. In this case, we surrender our ability to set our compass. Without a compass, we wander aimlessly through the desert of struggle; no, this desert doesn't have a magical genie that will whisk us away on a magic carpet ride to a "whole new world" where we are suddenly back on our own path either.

Your compass will be a valuable tool for your journey towards mastering struggle.

Do not rush the process of self discovery. Take your time exploring your strengths and areas of opportunity. Your compass is an internal safe haven when you feel lost. It helps build your strength and offers shelter in the shitstorm life throws at you.

FOUR POINTS

Your **north** is set to experiences, education, and people that will help you solidify your true north, or your true self. (Dare I call your "north" your authentic self?) Here you want to spend the most time asking questions, challenging the "norms," and sitting with your thoughts.

Accept wisdom from others in this area with *caution*: There is plenty of marketing targeting our pain and struggle to convince us that our north resides in the materialistic possessions and high-end experiences to which only the most "committed" are privy. Lies such as these play to our ego and our social identification. And acceptance, after all, is a large motivator for how we live our lives. It is also the source of a great deal of struggle that we will explore later in this book.

Our north can take the longest to identify, but it is also the factor that, if off by even the smallest percentage, can send us down a skewed path of purpose. This is why seeing the full compass can help create a clearer definition of what "north" means to us.

Take your **southern** directional point. This is your spiritual influence. This point is impacted by your beliefs, understanding, and connections to consciousness bigger than yourself. It doesn't ask for a religious practice, but it does require you to evaluate your deepest belief systems. The roots of your beliefs will profoundly shape where your north points. Think about it: *North would have no value if there were no south*—just as the dark would be irrelevant if there were no such thing as light. Contrast deepens understanding. Take your deepest beliefs, and ask how these beliefs shape the person you want to be.

The **eastern** needle moves by the influence of external environments and experiences. This area of your compass will be tied to things outside of yourself. When you look at these external forces, you will find an internal footprint. Your access to education may have been limited, and therefore you see struggle in learning. When someone is deprived of the basic tools of education, how can we expect them to harness the internal power to overcome this? But we do. We ask students from lower-income cities and suburbs with no access to books or healthy learning environments to rise up. Therefore, some students internalize that they are uneducated or unteachable as a result of this experience.

The external environments and experiences of the east play a part in leading your **western** directional point, which is where we harness true wisdom. *Wisdom emerges from experience.* Not all wisdom is good. If the eastern point of your compass is broken by pain and suffering, your wisdom can reflect deeper bitterness and cynicism. The internal footprint becomes a permanent tattoo that cannot be scrubbed off. A cycle of struggle with no hope of changing direction becomes the new normal.

As a college instructor for many years, I saw students from diverse backgrounds. I watched as many stood unaware of their compass, or not knowing how to fix the directions that had been broken. Their teachers, mentors, and coaches always shared the same rainbow sentiment: "I had the power to change anything I wanted to."

They didn't recognize that reality dictates this to be true only if a person has a compass that is intact and intentionally created.

BROKEN COM-PASS

I was one of those students whose compass was broken. My broken compass wasn't going to miraculously point north just because I held it in my hand and said, "Point north!" I had to study and struggle to find the teachers who could help me gain the skills I needed to fix my compass.

The process takes time and patience. It also takes careful observation of other people's struggles to help build upon our mastery of struggle's great complexity. Viewing struggle from one angle does not provide a complete picture, nor does it fill out the smaller directional points of your compass.

My first opportunity in my education to experience an alternative perception of struggle came when my high school student council did an "exchange program" with an inner city school. When I had to go through a metal detector and be patted down for weapons, as well as share a tattered book with three other classmates, my "well-off" high school perception of educational struggle changed.

When I first showed up, I saw students acting out and being disruptive, just like the teachers at the head of the classroom did. But when I left, I saw students hungry for equality in education. Students were tired of being brushed aside and treated like misfit toys. North wasn't even an option for them—it had been broken off their compasses completely. South was something these teens saw as a path belonging to their parents and grandparents. The only part of the compass they could relate to, or work through, was experience. Yet experience was so rough on them that it closed off their hopes for a north worth chasing.

OPPORTUNITY KNOCKING

If it feels like your compass is shattered, and you haven't found the right teachers to help you reset it, *this* is your opportunity. You cannot take back the past. You can't right the past wrongs of inequality that you have experienced, or the distorted beliefs you have passively observed. You will have to get your compass out and take a look at it: *Where does it need mending? Where does it need my attention?*

The student who was given an unfair shake in education unlocks struggle by recognizing that broken piece of the compass. So can you, but if and when you do, try not to linger in all the darkness.

It's easy to be consumed by bitterness and anger; it might still be fresh in your mind. Or you could currently be in that directional struggle. So my advice to you is: *Be present. Take notes. Don't play victim to it. Don't belittle its value either.*

I keep a journal on my desk, and each week I write one lesson gleaned from each directional point of my compass in it. *What is one thing I have learned from external experiences this week? What is a piece of wisdom I have gained? How have my beliefs deepened? And what is one way in which I feel closer to who I want to be?*

After six months, it was amazing what I experienced: I began to notice patterns in my thinking that were holding me back, and strength potential in areas I had never even considered. I now intentionally sought teachers who would challenge me. I started to listen to radio stations and read articles by people with whom I strongly disagreed—and I didn't do it to become more argumentative. I didn't do it to build my ego. *I used it to expose areas of my compass that still needed to be filled in.*

I also let go of my long-held belief that purpose was written in the stars—that my compass came complete with my north predetermined. I started to find my northwest and southeast points. I found how experiences and beliefs bled into one another, or how wisdom empowered my calling and purpose. I began to mend my broken compass by filling in all the dots around my north and letting purpose's picture become clearer in its time.

ON COURSE

Being your own guru does not mean closing yourself off to the wisdom, experiences, or people around you. It's about *filtering the information we receive and applying it to our internal compass.* This gives us a greater sense of our life's direction.

For many, our needles are spinning out of control, like a broken compass with no gravitational pull. By inserting someone of a similar education, upbringing, and passion's compass into your life, you skew your most important directional point: true north. One degree of miscalculation doesn't seem like much if it was just for a small walk or journey. But imagine a lifetime of one degree of miscalculation in your life. The entire journey is blown off course, and you end up lost in the woods.

Naturally, when we get to this point, we want to retrace our steps and find where we got off track. But if you have spent most of your life off course, you won't remember where that point even is anymore. Plus, you end up reliving the same mistakes and hardships twice, because you are walking the same path that made you get lost in the first place. Our vulnerability here leads us back to the wolf disguised as dear old Granny. And he keeps feeding us the "answers" that fatten us up for him.

Instead of retracing your steps, if you find yourself lost—STOP. *It's time to take an inventory of your life and ask how you got to this point.* Don't judge it. Why? Because you'll end up beating yourself up over your choices, which isn't productive if you want to move forward to assess where you are now.

Then *ask what you want your life to look like.* Take actions that move you closer to that goal. Seek advice and experiences that pull you closer to your dreams, and challenge your way of thinking.

Lean into the struggle, then learn from it. Become your own guru. This is your space to question, push the limits, and release.

Make sure you look at your map and compass now and again, so you don't get lost.

Chapter 4

UNIQUELY UNQUALIFIED

*"You don't understand anything
until you learn it more than one way."*

—MARVIN MINSKY

THROUGHOUT MY EDUCATION, I ENCOUNTERED TEACHERS WHO believe there is only one way to solve a problem—and especially my tenth-grade Honors Algebra II teacher. She would give us zero credit for any solution solved differently than the way she explained it in class.

This frustrating rule imposed on me deflated my interest in math. Not to mention, it also deflated my grade. How do we fully understand or master anything if we only approach it from one point of view?

I don't think we really can.

When I look at all the degrees, certifications, conferences, and experiences I have gone through in my life, I wondered why I never received my Ph.D. in struggling. If four years and 180 credit hours can get me a Bachelor of Science degree, why couldn't I receive my Ph.D. after thirty-plus years of life education in struggle?

I started studying struggle when I was nearly seven years old (without even realizing it). My father's death at that time was the catalyst for others seeing my expertise in an area I could hardly spell. Struggle became the Rosetta stone for unlocking the hidden, unspoken languages of human beings all around me. My friends began sharing their deeply personal tragedies with me. Sure, a goldfish dying wasn't exactly the same as the loss I felt from my father passing—but pain, adversity, and suffering were connecting me to the world.

So I started listening much more closely when my mother and aunts talked about life situations. I was glued to talk shows like Oprah, because of the invaluable life lessons discussed.

I also became enamored by the book *Harriet the Spy*, because she kept a diary of everything going on in her neighborhood. I wasn't exactly kid detective, but I did start journaling at a very young age about everything I saw and experienced. It didn't matter what I was observing; I recorded it all.

Whether it was a kid using a magnifying glass to burn ants (cruel) or two siblings arguing, struggle was universal, and I jotted down my observations of it. The journal was where I kept my observations. While many of those closest to me today would find it hard to believe I kept quiet about anything, struggle silenced me. I became its quiet student and it my most humbling teacher—with exception to my Organic Chemistry professor in college. A peculiar observation of this student-teacher relationship I had with struggle was what kept me silent about that study.

NEVER ENOUGH

It wasn't until recently that I realized just how long I have spent studying the matter of struggle, or how much I have to say. I realize what held me back was the feeling of being uniquely unqualified to ever share my knowledge. Psychologists call this "imposter syndrome." It's where you believe you are unqualified, and that you will be exposed as a fraud. But who could possibly call me out as being unqualified in the study of struggle, as all of us have varying levels of degrees in struggle?

The matters which deem us "qualified" for education and careers seem arbitrary—until you are lying on a hospital bed and asked to mark the part of your body that needs to be operated on. It's in that moment that you value your medical team's level of skill and education. And as you are lying on the sterile table in an operating room and asked to breathe deeply into a mask, you hope that you did your due diligence when finding the right surgeon for your procedure.

Or perhaps you have never been in that scenario at all. But I'll bet you have waited at a fast food restaurant, wondering if the teenager behind the counter is qualified enough to hear you say that you wanted no tomato, mayo, or pickles, and praying to God that he heard you say, "No bun." The gluten would turn you into a puffer fish, and you are just really hungry and hoping your order is right. (Does that sound a little more relatable?)

Whenever I speak in front of crowds or teach a class on the road, I feel uniquely unqualified. I begin questioning my credentials and experiences, convinced that someone will find out I'm a fraud, even though there are plenty of institutions, degrees, certifications, and logbooks full of evidence that I am more than qualified. I just... never quite get over the struggle of feeling as though I am not enough. That my experiences aren't enough. Hell, that my *struggles* aren't enough.

Have you ever gone into work ready to share the epic tale of your failure of a weekend, all because you didn't get to do your beach run, only to have your tongue make a complete U-turn as your peer shares the passing of a loved one with you? You immediately begin the comparison game and think, *Wow, I am not going to share my struggle. Compared to what Andy is going through, my struggle seems downright ridiculous.*

This example is simple, but we have all had moments where someone shares something deeply personal, and we frantically search our brain for any experience that seems remotely similar to prove (on some deeply twisted internal level) that we, too, understand struggle and pain. Comparison becomes the letter grade on the report card, and our G.P.A. displays the level of expertise we carry in this particular semester.

I mean, how bad is it that I can't even struggle properly?

SKIN THE CAT

As I look back at all the tiny little struggles along my life, I realize there were some that didn't even show up on my radar at the time because I was viewing other struggles that took high precedence first.

As for struggles that repeatedly showed up in my life, I felt like screaming, *I already DID this one; can I PLEASE move forward?*

To which life shouted back: "Maybe if you **address** the actual struggle this time, you can learn something, and then we would happily move forward with you. We aren't psyched about this *Groundhog Day* repeat you are having either."

There are fleeting moments of clarity that come to me. Those moments usually occur in vast, green-covered, ocean-spraying, sun-shining retreat locations; or they are quiet moments of stillness in the middle of my bedroom chanting. But the understanding is always the same: *There is beauty in the repeated struggle because it offers the opportunity for me to see it from a different perspective.* I know that reads like some serious optimistic bullshit, but if I couldn't put a little optimism into the learning process, I would drown in the heaviness of its lessons.

The perspectives build my résumé of struggle and give me more tools to draw from. Rather than feeling uniquely unqualified, I find my mindset shifting into feeling overly qualified, and I become embarrassed to be known as a master in this field. Who would, after all, want to be known as a "Struggle Guru?" It implies that shit has been so bad in my life that I am probably more messed up than you. And maybe that *is* exactly why you picked up this book in the first place: You can't help but continue to be drawn to something and someone in a situation that might be a little shittier than yours. Because let's face it, it feels a little better to know you aren't the only one fucking up at life.

But the name is quite misleading, because it implies that I am *your* guru. And I am most certainly not your guru—let alone your Struggle Guru. So why are you reading this book, and why am I wasting these pages with struggles that don't contain all the solutions?

Because there is more than one way to skin a cat. Your perspective, and my perspective, which includes thirty-plus years of other people's perspectives as well, are rolled into this work. This book lays out a path for others to continue to weave in their perspective and grow a community of Struggle Gurus who can change the world by offering an integrated and collaborative life study of struggle. So it's about hope and strength in our pain and suffering.

We need an army of gurus, and I hope that you can let go of feeling uniquely *un*qualified in the struggles of your life to see the value in your life experiences.

Seeing your struggles as education and experiences is the easy step. Owning it in front of others—well, that's some scary shit.

Chapter 5

A BAD CASE OF AUTHENTICITY

"Authenticity requires a certain measure of vulnerability, transparency, and integrity."

—JANET LOUISE STEPHENSON

IN DAVID SHANNON'S BOOK, *A BAD CASE OF STRIPES*, A YOUNG GIRL, Camilla, becomes so consumed with how others perceive her that she keeps changing the color of the stripes on her skin based on what everyone else calls her.

Camilla and I are pretty similar. The fear of being left out or bullied because of the person I was led to many shape-shifting transformations for me.

While many of my friends went through the pains of puberty hopeful for an after-school special movie moment where the ugly duckling becomes the swan, I was afraid that someone would find out that *this* ugly duckling was actually an otter with a duck costume on. Feelings of fear, scrutiny, and loss of friendship had me diving deep into the world of chameleon-style living. Just like Camilla, I would shape-shift into whatever others needed me to be as a way to hide the person I feared others knowing.

Participating in countless sports, student organizations, and volunteer programs kept my mind busy from wandering down the path of exploring who I was and how I was feeling while pretending to be this other person. My high school romances were an absolute flop, but it felt more normal to "be involved" and dating than to be single.

Struggle began to bury my true self deep within me, and fear became sadness. Sadness became depression, because being different in a children's book (*A Bad Case of Stripes*) is vastly different than being different in real life: That book's happy endings and easily digestible lessons are not a realistic reflection of how humans experience being different.

Could the person I really was be so awful that it was worth all of this pain? Or was struggle leading me down a path of loneliness for no reason?

It wasn't until college, when I was "on my own," so to speak, that I met others who bravely stood in their truth. But even their truth was covered in painted threads of others similar to them. Few were "authentic"—until I met a mentor in college who changed the meaning of the word "authentic" for me and helped me find the words to say what I had hidden from the world for so long: "I am gay."

PIECE OF THE PUZZLE

Amy is a quietly brilliant woman, both in speech and humbleness. You wouldn't realize she had a master's degrees and a Ph.D. She is an advocate for every student she meets, and works diligently to leave this world better than she found it. I admire everything about her.

It took just one meeting with Amy as a resident assistant to feel this overwhelming calm come over me. Her presence made me feel at home in my thoughts and body. I didn't feel judgment or fear. It was just *easy*. I could be me.

What *wasn't* easy was owning my truth. I still remember standing in the bathroom on the second floor of my dorm. I can still see the pale yellow paint chipped around the sink I was standing at as I looked into the mirror and said, "Kirsten, you are gay." After saying those words, I paused, shook my head, and said again, "I am gay." Then I promptly ran to the bathroom stall and threw up. All of the calm and acceptance that Amy had shown me were not enough to take away the fear that boiled up within me at that moment. The floodgates of being a Christian, my sexuality being a sin, and the idea of family, friends, and peers knowing made me throw up yet again. Tears rushed down my face—perhaps mostly because my face was near a college dorm room toilet, and that's not a place where anyone wants to be.

The angel on my shoulder said, "You worry too much. It will be fine."

The devil cackled, "It's been nice knowing you. You will lose everything now. Kiss your life goodbye."

How could something that I see as just *one* piece of the million-piece puzzle that makes me who I am, be the missing piece that always seems to fall on the floor; the one that you can never find, but screws up the whole damn puzzle?

DOUBLE LIFE

That's when I started to live two lives: The life-in-college me where I only surrounded myself with other people who were gay, and the hometown me, the Kirsten who played it straight.

I'm not entirely sure what this sea change meant, but I did know that the double life was making me a liar.

Making up hangouts and friends—just to meet someone in whom I was interested—snowballed quickly.

Weirdly, I knew even less about who I was now that I had "come to terms" with my identity. *How could this be possible?* Two seconds before, I had been jumping out of a closet with rainbows and unicorns, and now here I was boarding up the closet, putting up drywall and brick to bury it forever. *Where was the "authentic" Kirsten now?*

I became a ball of emotions going through the motions of day-to-day life but never admitting my truth. And when I eventually opened up to one close friend, she said, "You know that you are going to hell?"

What? Could an all-loving God who made me, one of His children, in His image, have made a mistake? Did He forget to add some hardwiring to my circuit board?

DIVING

I dove deeply into Jesus. No, really: I joined the Campus Crusade for Christ, which the kids on campus called "The Dive." I thought I just needed to be a better Christian. I thought I could "pray the gay away" if I kept my head down and followed.

Do you know what I also told myself? *Stop being so selfish. There are people in this world with real struggle and pain.*

I continued with my studies, but I also applied to seminary at Duke, Vanderbilt, and Yale. I was going to be a missionary. Travel the world and bury myself in guilt of others' pain and suffering to drown out my own. That should cure the gay.

Accepted to all three colleges, I was overjoyed—but deeply saddened at the same time. I had prayed, "If it is Your will for me to do this missionary work, give me a sign." The sign of those three acceptance letters might as well be the Holy Trinity itself conspiring to lead me down the religious (and falsely believed) righteous path.

An encounter with my church youth pastor would change my seminary trajectory completely.

CONTAGIOUS

I had been working as a youth leader for seventh-grade boys, and the truth about my sexual orientation was discovered—the details aren't important. So I was asked to meet with the youth pastor. He told me that parents were concerned with their children being led by a gay youth leader; they feared I might "turn them."

These same parents take their kids to Starbucks every day, but no one seems too concerned that their child might become a latte. But gay is different. Clearly, it's contagious.

I wanted to speak to the senior pastor about the situation, but feared that he, too, would feel that way. I truly looked up to my senior pastor—he was a huge reason behind why I wanted to go to seminary—but still I couldn't look him in the eye and tell him who I was. The rejection would have been too much.

So I distanced myself. I hid from him, my family, the world.

AUTHENTICITY

No doubt this is where you are waiting for the moment where I came out to my family and friends, and things turned around. But they didn't at first.

When I came out, I was not received with open arms. I was pushed out and shut out. Potential employers denied me employment out of fear. Friends abandoned me because of clichés and misconceptions.

Being authentic isn't a catchy hashtag or social media thread. Authentic has nothing to do with athleisure wear, coffee, and master class seminars. *Authentic is gritty and dirty*. It's standing as you are, and letting the world throw shit at you, but still refusing to move. Authentic isn't about popularity, or following; it's about living in the world as only *you* can. It requires embracing the loneliness of the journey at times. But celebrating its growth at other moments.

Struggling with my sexuality made me an outcast, but it also filled my lungs with more meaningful breath. I wasn't breathing in the secondhand smoke of other people's bullshit that was neatly packaged to morph me into their clone. I was breathing the full, free air of my authentic self. She might have enemies, she might not have the support of the world, but she is freer than former Kirsten ever was.

Authenticity requires vulnerability and transparency; that is clear. And what I lost in the process, I gained back in strength and wisdom. Some who claimed to be close friends never came back once I'd come out. *But family and friends who were just as unsure of what it all meant, came back stronger and filled me with a love I didn't know I could experience.*

If you are struggling with the person you are, you aren't alone. Your path might be different; the emotions and experiences are unique. People don't share in the price of authenticity. It's quite easy for others looking from the outside in to assume and judge the process. The rainbow flags, parades, and celebrations can be a painful reminder of the hopes we have in moments of being our authentic self. The media portrays the glitter at the end of the struggle but glosses over the internal war that is tearing us apart. It hurts to believe that rising above the struggle could cost us relationships, careers, or experiences that we hold so sacred to us. It would be understandable to want to let myself become the chameleon and blend in just to numb the pain.

This is where uniting as Struggle Gurus is more important than ever. When you give voice to your story, that could help other people dig themselves out from under the boulder of emotion that is crushing their spirit. Surrounding yourself with people who love you, ALL of you, helps disperse the heavy load of struggle and gives you time to heal.

I try to remind myself that there will always be a critic to judge. There will always be someone who will misunderstand me or try to warp my authenticity into something to fit their beliefs and agenda. This wisdom helps me remove the weight of their judgment from my shoulders. After all, their judgment was a load I was never intended to carry. Sometimes, even just saying the words, "This is not my load to carry," frees my thoughts to focus on the aspects of my life that matter most instead of tying them up in people, experiences, and situations that do not matter.

It can feel just as foreign being your true self—your north— as it did when you walked the earth as your false self.

The process of authenticity is not linear. It's not like milestones and developmental ages that tell you the event should happen.

You might not be ready to share with the world all that you are. Don't let anyone rush that process. You may choose to share with some, and it may be enough in that moment. Or you may be ready to share the person you are with the world. When the cost of what you will gain outweighs what you fear you will lose, you will know the time is right. *Until that moment comes, the struggle continues to build your growth.*

Chapter 6

THE POWER OF BEING SEEN

*"At times I have struggled to feel seen, to have my history feel seen,
to have where I come from feel seen because I 'turned out great.'
But that doesn't mean that I Am Fine. I am working every day,
tirelessly, like you wouldn't believe, on being fine."*

—LANE MOORE

"I SEE YOU." THREE OF THE MOST POWERFUL WORDS ANOTHER human can hear. I argue that "I see you" is even more powerful than "I love you." "I love you" feels conditional in the many ways it is delivered or expressed. Saying "I see you" is the deepest level of love that surrenders the boundaries of conditional love and extends it into the infinite. It seems a shame that these words feel more fictional than practical, more cinematographic than deeply personal. Worse… how little we inquire of its power to connect the dots of our internal compass or unlock the power of struggle's true nature.

In my own journey, I believed my most authentic energy, not just the body that contains this energy, was not seen because I denied a primal element of my humanity—my sexual orientation. It turned out that sharing this aspect of myself did not free me, nor did it clear the path for me to finally be seen. In many ways it felt like I had just piled on new labels and new struggles. This lack of visibility required that I become more creative in how I drew attention to myself.

When I recall the groups of people, careers, and choices I made to try and be seen, I am sick to my stomach over some of my choices. I couldn't see in that moment all the ways I was compromising who I was, just to be seen. I would rather be seen by someone than carry the loneliness I was feeling in my heart. The time of being seen would vary from group to group and situation to situation. If I needed to be "more gay" to be seen, by golly, I would gay it up. If I needed to be "management" material, I would step up my professional game. Anything that was necessary in order to be seen. Sometimes conforming aesthetically or professionally wasn't enough. I started to look too much like everyone else, so I had to find a way to differentiate myself. I would observe the groups I was around long enough to see the leader they wanted, and then I would insert my opinions and ideas to fit their agenda. I wouldn't just be seen; by God, I would be heard.

Regardless of the arena, I would insert my "well-intended" input as a way to assert my presence and relevance. I'm tearing up writing this truth. It still stings to think of my not all that much younger self just struggling to be seen. There are still days when that young woman tries to rear her head; her innocent and youthful understanding of her ego was manipulating her. The longer I denied the truth, the more struggle presented itself. If I wanted to align with my authentic self, I needed to be vulnerable and start taking ownership of my choices.

You might not like this part, but you are the only one who can take ownership of your actions. It's not your parents' fault for not raising you better or your boss's for not seeing your potential. Rage may be building up inside of you as you read what appears to be my self-imposed judgment of your personal situation. Truth is a hard pill to swallow. I am not arguing the struggle of your upbringing or the ungratefulness of your boss, but I do argue that you play a role in every aspect of your life. It's your life after all. You are still the leading character. Sitting with choices you have made means looking at failures and extracting the lessons. It requires an openness to what it reveals and an ownership of these truths. I hated admitting that many of my life choices centered around denying how much I wanted to be seen. I'm not the only person who lives this way. In fact, I believe it's what all of us desire. It's the actions taken to be seen that differ. There are some, whom I admire, who find purpose early in their life and feel empowered to use this purpose to be seen. There are others who are seen early in life, and as a result, engage in opportunities that amplify their ability to not only be seen but heard.

I didn't fit into either of those groups. I felt invisible. I chose to participate in activities that came easy and gave me a platform to be seen. As that opportunity faded, so did my visibility. I would cling to the next event or person who saw me and continue this cycle over and over.

I even blamed a distant relationship with my mother on her not seeing me. I thought, as my mother, she should've been able to see me before anyone else, including myself. I subconsciously assigned the role of my "seen"-ness to her. When that didn't materialize, I found more subconscious ways to justify why she didn't understand me. I projected my inability to ask the most difficult questions of my presence on her motherhood. It was unjust and strained our relationship. I couldn't expect her to accept me with open arms or guide me through any of my life trials when I couldn't even be honest about who I was and what it meant to be seen by her or the rest of the world.

The confusion over what it means to be seen gets tangled up with narcissism or "celebritism." It's not about thinking so highly of yourself or feeling so entitled to the purpose you possess that you ignore others. It is the founding idealism of the Sanskrit word "Namaste." More than a way to close a yoga practice or a T-shirt slogan, it means "The Light in me acknowledges the Light within you." Put another way, "I see you, because I also see me." It's not oneness; it's wholeness. It's not individuality; it's unity. I want to be seen beyond the flesh, beyond my acts of kindness or service, beyond my clothing choices or life partner. I want the energy of a higher vibration within me to be felt and move in such a way that it also allows me to feel the vibration of every living thing on this earth.

The blind can still see, the deaf can still hear, the paraplegic can still feel. The senses mean more than the physical world can explain, and being seen is more than the physical. It's exactly why it is the magnetic pull that moves our compass. It guides us toward struggles that directly impact the part of our compass that needs our attention the most. Struggle isn't keeping you from being seen. Struggle works with "seen" to direct your life. Wrap your mind around this idea, and your head will begin to spin. The first real shift in struggle's role in my life was seeing its partnership with my greatest desires.

Have you stopped to think of struggle as working with you?

Does the very idea of it being on your side go against everything you have been taught or conditioned to believe? I understand. It feels like a trick of some dark force trying to convert
you to the dark side. Turn inward for a moment and let yourself
be vulnerable. What does it mean for you to be seen? How does
being seen manifest itself in your relationships, work, community, friendships, spiritual growth? Make a list of each of these
and ask yourself if you feel seen. If the answer is yes, in what
ways are you seen in this role? Is this how you want to be seen?
If the answer is yes, wonderful, gold star for you. More than
likely, there will be some "noes". Where you said no, it's time to
ask if you are trying to be seen in this place or relationship as a
placeholder for another space where you really want to be seen.
If you are conforming, like Camilla in *A Bad Case of Stripes*, it's
time to step back. It might even be time to let go. Or at the very
least to start looking at an alternative path. No one said you
have to jump ship when you can clearly see the iceberg is 20
miles ahead. Charting a new path isn't a bad idea, though.

Take ownership of your choices, but also be gentle with
their results. We are not perfect and will not make perfect
choices going forward with this knowledge either. Beating
yourself up with guilt and shame over how you came to this
point in your journey devalues the person you are. The person
you are picked up this book, which is a recognition of change.
That person is someone who isn't afraid to learn from mistakes
and ask for directions when they feel lost on the path.

I know that when you picked up this book, you may not
have felt seen. These words may strike such a familiar chord that
it makes you uneasy. The struggle of being seen may be one
you will wrestle with for some time. Being seen takes effort. It
takes practice. It requires us to show up in our lives every single

day. Be present with the good as well as the bad. Rather than lingering in the ways we are not seen, we change our mindset to one that takes a different path. You don't keep going down the path that is wrong. Instead, you switch paths, you move in the direction that gets you closer to your goals. If you want to stand on top of the mountain and be seen, learn to enjoy the journey. Laugh now and again at all the crazy ways you stumble. I know I have. I have stumbled, tumbled, and landed face first in a pile of horse manure, and all I can do is laugh at the absurdity of the moment. The humanness of me also has moments of complete fits and rage. Sometimes those fits take me off course, and a couple have even sent me nearly over the edge. I show up anyway.

The ability to really be seen occurred for me when I stopped trying so hard to shout, "Look at me," and I drew inward. I asked myself over and over how I wanted to be seen. The path started to build itself. I wanted to have a larger impact in therapeutic yoga practices and less presence in bootcamps, so I began researching and developing practices that were more in line with my desire. I slowly integrated small practices into my weekly classes, and concepts into workshops or seminars I taught at, to gauge the interest. I knew I was being seen when others connected with the energy I brought through my research and thoughtful practices. I didn't have to be funny, flashy, or gimmicky in my presentation. I showed up, presented the energy I created, and sat back to feel the vibration I felt from others.

I realize how new age this sounds, and it might feel like too much for you as a reader, but I am okay with that. That's part of my ability to stay strong in being seen. The recognition that not everyone will connect to my vibration. It's exactly why I am calling you to hone your own energy. Your energy will resonate with others' that mine cannot reach. Their energy will connect with some that you cannot reach. And so on and so forth. It magnifies infinitely, and soon the world is being moved by the power of individuals who live in a space of being seen.

Help others be seen. There is a world of people crying out to be seen—lost, hurt, broken. I know I have identified with all of these. Sometimes the burden of unearthing what it means to be seen is too great. Perhaps, the people we love the most abandon us in the process. You don't know where someone is coming from. You don't know their pain or struggles. But you can speak from a space of understanding that, ultimately, we all just want to be seen.

Chapter 7

OCEAN TIDES

*"Having anxiety and depression is like being scared
and tired at the same time. It's the fear of failure, but no urge
to be productive. It's wanting friends, but hating to socialize.
It's wanting to be alone, but not wanting to be lonely.
It's feeling everything at once and then feeling paralyzingly numb."*

—ANONYMOUS

THE OCEAN LOOKED CALM, ALMOST GLASSLIKE, AS THE SUN BEGAN to peek out over the horizon. The stillness was inviting and drew me closer.

I slid off my boots and let the icy cold water inch up on shore and light up the nerve endings on my feet as the water rushed over them. Part of me wanted to retreat, while another challenged me to embrace the feeling even further. Paralyzed by the decision to exit the frigid water or inch myself deeper into its icy lesson, I stared blankly at the ocean.

A couple walking through the six inches of snow on the beach behind me began to shout something that I could not understand. Their words were muffled by the ocean mixing with the wind that had begun to pick up.

The woman rushed up to me, grabbed me, and then pulled me back from the ocean edge. "Are you *crazy*? That water isn't more than thirty-seven degrees. You could get hypothermia or freeze to death if you go out there."

I continued to stare blankly.

Her face softened as she realized the harsh words were not penetrating the internal dialogue running through my head. She shifted her questioning to a softer "Are you okay?"

I nodded, and she reluctantly began to walk back to her companion.

We both knew I wasn't okay, and as they shuffled their feet and tried to play off their limited progress forward and away from me, I remained still.

I may speak of visibility and wanting to be seen, but when depression and anxiety crept into my thoughts, I crawled back into the hole where I only wanted to be invisible to the world.

Mental health is not a topic we discuss publicly. It closets those struggling as much as being gay hid me behind closet doors for most of my adolescence. We know it exists and that it's not a choice, but we still label and talk down to many struggling with it.

When you are mentally ill, shame and guilt pile onto the fear and anxiety. The entire experience steals your words and blocks your emotions. Feeling muted and unseen makes you feel like you are being dragged by the undertow of the ocean. Here you are walking along feeling good, and *BAM! You are pulled under*. Frantically waving your hands and fighting the current, you take in what feels like gallons of water. You try to conserve energy, so you stop waving your hands, but only sink faster. People above the surface sound garbled, like Charlie Brown's schoolteacher shouting, "Keep fighting!"

To me it seems there is a misunderstanding—because I *haven't* given up the fight—but I don't know how to make it back to the surface. I am paralyzed by the choices in front of me, unsure of the "right" option because no one prepared me for how this would feel, much less how to fight and combat it.

ONE IN A BILLION

I have read enough self-help books, spoken to enough counselors, and enrolled in enough seminars and fitness programs to know what fighting is not.

It is not a simple solution perfectly packaged in a five-step program or a ten-week training plan. It isn't just taking medication and channeling more positive thoughts.

Such "coping" devices are well-intentioned, but they trivialize the root of the struggle. Their program is for them, not me.

What if I am the one in a billion people this program or process doesn't work for, because they aren't ME? What if it only works for people exactly like them? And even if I am one of those, what happens when I do everything you say, but continue to drown?

Oh, right, just read the next book and go to the next meeting.

I wished that someone who had struggled with depression and anxiety and found a way to manage could have sat with me. I wished they would cut the bullshit and lecture series to tell me, "Depression is not something you can *cure*. You will spend the rest of your life learning new tools and means to recognize it and manage its grasp on you."

I don't "buy into" my depression and anxiety being cured. And you can disagree: I'm sure someone with more credentials and experience will argue my ignorance. But this is my story, my struggle. You cannot diminish my experiences as invalid; even the Ph.D. and the medical doctor knows that.

Here is what I've gleaned; here is some of my experience: *Nature gives us ways in which to learn not just about its healing, but also about how we can heal ourselves.*

Let's return to the beach. Although the day is different, I am finding that there are many lessons to learn about struggle in this vast sea.

The sun was shining, and the ocean waves appeared to be rolling perfectly for this novice surfer. I met up with friends, and we engaged in a private surf lesson. We learned everything our instructor could tell us about standing up on the board before he set us free: "Go ahead, paddle out and then just catch a wave."

Wow, was that it? Just catch a wave and stand up? Why hadn't I thought of that?

This oversimplification of the surf process did not set any of us students up for success. Since we were missing the waves, our instructor strategically stayed in the water behind us and, when he saw a wave he liked for one of us, pushed one of us forward on our board and yelled, "Pop up!!"

I had absolutely no clue as to why he thought that a particular wave was perfect for me and not one of my friends. *What clues is the ocean giving him that let him know?* When I asked, he responded, "You just know."

Great. Another useless tool for helping me study the waves.

This is what I see in the wellness community when it comes to mental health: "Are you struggling with depression? Just do yoga, and it will go away."

Great. I'll do that. But why?
The response is usually, "Because it worked for me."
What it doesn't tell me is how or why it would do the same for me.

OBSERVATION

I went out into the ocean and separated myself from the group. I sat on my board and observed other experienced surfers as they sat on their boards and began to feel the rhythm of the ocean. I began to mimic them, and the process heightened my awareness to what I was feeling in my body. I caught one or two waves on my own, and as I paddled back out, I started to think about what was similar among those waves that let me know a wave was "right" for me.

When I rode the waves, I would get rolled left and right, walk too close to the nose of the board, and flip, or walk too far back and "bog." But *every failure was a new opportunity to find what worked specifically for ME.* I still failed to catch the perfect wave at times, but I became far more successful at observing all the tiny, subtle ways in which the ocean was cuing me to stand up and ride the wave.

As I continued to observe others more experienced in riding the waves, I studied as much of the ocean as possible. My "perfect" wave would never be quite the same as any of the others—and there was nothing wrong with that at all.

COMPLEXITY

Paddling out into the ocean of my thoughts, I discovered that every day was different, and the ways I coped with depression and anxiety might not work one year, or hell, even a week from now! That didn't mean I was broken, unfixable, or not trying hard enough.

I began to see that *when the ways in which I managed my depression were no longer working, it was usually because I had outgrown them.*

At one point, physical activity was the only way to work through my anxiety and depression; now I need more stillness and quiet. I adapt better and am able to surface faster when I carve out quiet moments to just let my body and mind be still.

My mind and body often would be running on all cylinders—and not necessarily in the same direction. Finding stillness allows me to reconnect and align.

It's worth noting that plenty of people misunderstand the complexity of a person's battle with mental health. If I had a dime for every time I opened myself up to tell someone I loved or trusted about what I was going through and they responded with, "Why don't you try therapy? Have you thought about running to work through depression? What about medication? You have to just dig in your heels and push a little harder, and it will get better," I would have a great retirement plan saved.

They could never see I was trying to do all of those things but still felt paralyzed by my battle. Worse than battling the illness was having every wellness guru and "influencer" on the planet tell me that they had the "magic cure."

Do your very best to not tangle more energy and emotion into their lack of experience or understanding of what you are dealing with.

UNDERTOW

There were moments I let thoughts creep in that were saying, *Why CAN'T you get better? Everyone else who has done this has, and they have even written a book about it!*

Ahh. There was the undertow I didn't see again, pulling me under, and filling my lungs with water; making it impossible to breathe. And every technique in the yoga handbook that I was ever taught didn't seem to offer me a way to take my practice off the mat and into the world that was sinking around me.

OXYGEN

It wasn't until years later that I met a teacher who could help me find my breath again. Lying on my back in the middle of a yoga teacher training in California, I soaked in my breath for the first time in a way I didn't know was possible. Breathing in through the nose and feeling the air move past my nostrils and down the back of my throat had this cleansing texture. It was as if I could feel the toxicity of my thoughts being absorbed in this oxygen-rich experience.

I felt parts of my body fill with air that I didn't know could expand, and when my teacher, Tiffany, told us to sigh out the breath, I swear I sighed out twenty years of shit. The back of my body began to get heavy, but not in the ways it had felt heavy in dark moments of my depression. It felt grounded, rooted, connected. My heart, not the chakra metaphysical one, but my actual heart, felt like it was beating in a new way. I knew I was skeptical too, of the "magic" of someone else's moment of relief.

But it didn't stop there. There was an exchange between my breaths that was a conversation with my body as well.

"I've got you."

I could hear it so clearly.

Until this moment, I thought relief was always someone else's to experience. I thought that I was the exception to the rule, and that some of my most trusted teachers growing up had sold me a lie.

IN THE WAVES

I may have taken my first real breath free of anxiety and depressive thoughts, but the battle was far from over. I wanted to dive deeper into the teachings of my breath as a way to help others, but found myself at odds with my qualifications. *Here I go again, feeling Imposter Syndrome trying to diminish my voice. There was doubt again, rearing its head, trying to tear down the value in my story.*

I thought that my battle with mental health problems might deem me unfit to help anyone else. But as I have progressed through many of life's struggles, I see that it is exactly this experience that makes me qualified to write this:

> I have no idea what your answer is, but you are not alone. I can give you the resources and support your exploration of the various modalities that could work for you, and be a sounding board when you are pissed off and frustrated over the many modalities that will fail you. And I will stand beside you to tell you that if the modality doesn't help solve the complex puzzle of your mind, you are NOT a failure. And that there are still more answers.
>
> Stick with it. That is what I can offer. It's not much, but it is the most authentic offer I have seen on the table in years.

So I'm not selling you a magic pill. Nor am I chastising you for not having found the answer yet. The journey is messed up, and there will be moments where you feel like you are being tossed in the ocean repeatedly. And the world will be all too swift to judge, and too slow to offer real help.

I AM

Much of my anxiety is rooted in thoughts that rip me out of the present. The thoughts are shortcomings of my past and fears of the future. As I studied what it means to be human, I had this awakening.

Follow me for a moment as I share this awakening with you; the wisdom has come from years of battling depression and anxiety.

Each of us are human beings—a universally undeniable fact. "Am" is the first person present singular of the verb "to be"—a single person speaking about themselves in the present. One might conclude that we are designed to be fully present from creation. If we are human beings, then our divine connection is in *the now*.

When I began to wrap my brain around the yoga principles I studied and meditated on for years, I realized that *part of my depression was feeling bound to the past*. I would refer to who I was, not am.

I could speak in circles for a lifetime on this principle, but it would not pull you or me out of depression any faster or simplify the depths of depression. But it can and does give me roots to this moment, and it gives me today to work on the thoughts and feelings that try to tear me to the past or future and darken my present.

Stripping back labels and exposing myself as "I am" is like exposing a fresh wound to saltwater. It burns and is painful. It leaves me feeling raw. And it brings in yet another layer of struggle with which to cope—and this time it feels like too much to bear.

So when my wave feels like it is growing larger, and the world is tossing me around, I close my eyes and repeat, *"I am."*

It doesn't reverse the depression, but it does force me to stop and be here *now*. To breathe deeply, let the salt hit the wound, and know that healing can take time. And, like with a surfer waiting for that "perfect wave," sometimes there are days and weeks with shitty sets.

Still, I don't stop surfing.

You too have to just keep showing up.

Be present and learn what it feels like when your wave arrives.

If you are as busy as "I was," or "I will be," you will never see or feel the wave come. You will get rolled like sushi and arrive to shore cut up, bruised, and even more broken than when you paddled out.

You don't have to let the waves control your life. You can learn from the fellow surfers around you and begin to develop your own "surf style."

The hardest step is shedding the labels tied to mental health and letting others give you a surf lesson.

Chapter 8

THE NALGENE DILEMMA

"Definitions belong to the definers, not the defined."

—TONI MORRISON

IF WE DIDN'T CALL A MAPLE TREE A MAPLE, WOULD IT KNOW ITS purpose? Could it still produce its sweet nectar and trickle down the rugged bark of its trunk? Would its branches cease to extend and move with the wind? Would it never bring shade to those who huddle beneath it on hot summer days? Who created the label "tree," anyway? Was it the tree, or did we as humans need to exert power over this living piece of nature and let it know exactly who we thought it was in this world?

The philosophical dilemma of this tree has roots much deeper than the maple. It is the basis for much of the struggle I have seen and experienced throughout my life. Shakespeare claims a rose by any other name would smell as sweet, and yet we label, categorize, and rank which words could live up to the sweetness of its smell or romantic symbolism of its blossoming.

I guess we need labels to help us establish position and power in our lives. How could I know that someone leads the company without CEO as their title? Or... could I not deduce they are probably the one in charge from the bags under their eyes, the Venti double-shot Americano on their desk, the incessant dinging of their phone reminding them of appointments and emails, or the general location of their office in relation to everyone else? Certainly, I would be less inclined to conclude the person pushing the broom with disheveled hair and visibly worn clothing is calling the shots.

We cling to the labels given to us when they afford us power, status, and influence. But just as quickly, we vault the labels that could make us feel inferior, weak, or God forbid, *different*.

You may think that not all labels are bad, because if all flatware were called a fork, and you were asked to "pass the fork," you might stare at the vast assortment of silverware with bewilderment, paralyzed by fear and embarrassed over the idea that you might select the wrong one.

But the labels I want to explore are the ones that interfere with our purpose. Maybe you read this and think, *I don't even know what my purpose is, so how can I begin to examine labels that impact this?* Let me explain using an example that is familiar to most. I've labeled it the Nalgene dilemma.

Labels are like stickers on a Nalgene water bottle. They start off as fun and seem to accent the bottle nicely. Too many stickers, however, can cover up the lid and render a water bottle useless.

Not long before the first sticker was ever placed on it, the Nalgene bottle was created with a divine (or perhaps capitalistic) purpose – to carry water. Its purpose was clear: It must hold liquids. One day, someone, somewhere thought that the multicolored water bottle was not enough, so they placed a sticker on the bottle. It was a sticker they had received from a friend and which they thought was really cool. They were super pumped to place it on something, and they chose this bottle as the perfect spot.

At first, the sticker helped differentiate the bottle from the millions of other Nalgene bottles. But it turned out that other people received the same sticker and also put it on *their* bottle. Now the water bottle looked just like thousands of others. So the person placed another sticker on the bottle to help separate it from the masses. But this sticker too was duplicated on other bottles, and so on and so forth.

After a while, the water bottle became completely encased in stickers. Its owner couldn't even open the lid, so no water could be put in to fill the bottle. The water bottle's purpose was negated because of all the stickers covering it.

Taking a couple of stickers off the lid is the easiest way to reclaim the water bottle's purpose. Unfortunately, peeling off a sticker that has been on a Nalgene bottle for some time leaves behind a sticky residue and remnants of the original sticker. Even if you tried to scrub off the label, the lid wouldn't close tightly and the water would constantly leak out.

Let's return to how this applies to us as humans.

LABELS

From birth, we have labels attached to us: girl, boy, athlete, nerd, genius, math whiz, musical prodigy, artist, and so forth. By the time we get to kindergarten, we have more labels than we have space on our water bottle!

Now, just imagine if you were able to determine your life-long labels by the time you were six years old—and you were given the choice of those label stickers to put on your Nalgene. When I was six, I would have covered my water bottle in Rainbow Brite, My Little Pony, Nickelodeon, and Disney everything.

But if you have ever watched a child dress themselves for the first time, you know that when a child is given options, they don't always turn out as expected. I mean, one time I tried to wear every single pair of my day-of-the-week underwear all at once, telling my mom I could just "… peel off the top pair each day instead of changing my underwear daily."

Have you figured out the problem in this scenario? Yep, the dirty underwear would be the last pair taken off at the end of the week. So… maybe predetermining every label we want for ourselves in kindergarten isn't the greatest idea.

As a child, I didn't understand that labels could even *be* bad until my father passed away, and I saw how people changed the way they spoke and interacted with my mom, now labeled "widow and single parent." This label was given to her; it wasn't her choice. Struggle gave it to her—and the community adjusted their interactions accordingly.

Now you might think they saw her as the Wonder Woman badass she really is, but the reality is they saw her as a Disney princess needing rescuing. No one thought she was capable of raising three young girls successfully. Even the church we went to told my mother she should give her kids up for adoption, so they could live a better life. ***What the French toast? Are you kidding me?***

My mother could have kept the label of "damsel in distress" the world wanted to give her, but she crumpled it up and tossed it. That label wasn't getting prime real estate on *her* Nalgene bottle.

I wasn't quite as strong as my mom. I caved to the pressure

of friends, teachers, and a sense of belonging. I let people slap stickers all over my bottle and never questioned them.

BURIED

Whether you realize it or not, you—indeed, all of us—have a divinely created purpose within you. But it's easy to lose sight of THAT purpose when you are caught up in—labels.

A lifetime can go by, until suddenly, one day you see all the residue of labels that you tore off, but that still have a grip on you. Or you stop trying to take them off at all, and just start covering them up with new ones, hoping it will "cover everything up." In the process, YOU get left behind. *Your purpose is buried, or covered up.*

Besides which, everyone tells you that if you just take *their* label, they will scrub all the others away for you. This feels too good to be true, and while rationally you know it's a scam, you give in anyway. It probably even works for a while, because with the sticker they throw in "community" and a sense of "belonging." But the cheap adhesive on their label eventually gives way—and your old label surfaces. Fear drives you to use any means possible to conceal the identity beneath all of the labels. You even try to tape and glue the new label back down to cover up the old label.

Conformity spirals you down a rabbit hole of lies. A divide deepens between you and your purpose, the truth of which can only be seen if you are willing to open the lid and fill up your bottle.

DEFINING SELF

Our purpose is the shadow of our authentic self. And just like in *Peter Pan*, our shadow can run away from us. We try to stick it back on with the stickers, but it still runs away from us.

When we spend so much time being all of these other things instead of being our true self, our purpose cannot be seen. It's like living in complete darkness with no sun: Our shadow is invisible. Not to say it's not there, but it cannot be seen.

In order to fully be seen, and to be visible, and to overcome the struggle of conformity, *we have to be careful as to how we label ourselves*.

Your authentic self isn't a hashtag or persona created for likes and follows. It's gritty and messy. It doesn't care what designer name is on your shirt or what exotic travels you have taken. *The authentic self sees its purpose long before the rest of the world can.*

When you see it, dress yourself up with labels that empower you to use your voice and rise up. Recognize that it's not the labels that are separating you from others; it's the purpose of your bottle (soul).

Today, shake up your bottle and see what contents bubble up. Scrub the labels that you feel have served their purpose to bring you to this point. Buy a bottle of Goo Gone and don't let the residue keep you bound to the past.

One more thing. **Don't change labels or rip them off because I told you to; who the hell am I to tell you to take them off or put more on?**

Doubt me, challenge me.

Throw this book across the room in a fit of rage over the absurdity of the analogy. But then, pick it back up and start asking yourself who lives beneath the stickers.

You are not defined by what others call you. Y*ou choose* how you are defined.

Chapter 9

ARCHITECTURAL GENES

"A man that has not dealt with his foundation
cannot deal with another man's foundation."

—STEVEN CHUKS NWAOKEKE

. . .

"Once we built structures entirely from the most durable substances we
knew: granite block, for instance. The results are still around today to
admire, but we don't often emulate them, because quarrying, cutting,
transporting, and fitting stone require a patience we no longer possess."

—ALAN WEISMAN, *THE WORLD WITHOUT US*

HISTORICAL ARCHITECTURAL STRUCTURES DRAW MILLIONS ACROSS the globe to admire their intricacies, fine craftsmanship, and visual depiction of patience and perseverance. The durability of the structure proves most appealing because we believe, perhaps on a subconscious level, that true works of art, even in the human form, are resilient and can stand the test of time. In humans, the ability to pass genetic traits to our offspring is one way in which we are able to express the tiniest details of beauty and durability of our heritage. But with the good genes also comes the erosion of the architecture: the genetic mutations, and predispositions to certain cancers, and the tendency toward male pattern baldness.

I studied advanced genetic courses in college, and I have closely examined the genetic architecture of my own family. I have both laughed in jest that the "lifeguard was off duty when one particular trait slipped in the gene pool" and shaken in fear when I read my test results positive for "BRCA1," a genetic marker that increases one's risk for breast, ovarian, pancreatic, cervical, uterine, and colon cancers. The architecture of DNA is intricate and complex. Yet the human genome varies slightly between all of us. How does the genetic makeup that is so similar among humans result in such varied struggles? Let's look at the architecture of the struggle.

Every house begins with a foundation. It is the lowest, load-bearing part of the building—the genetic makeup of our being in this metaphor. The foundation is built in the same way for everyone. It requires a shared DNA between a sperm and an egg. Not everyone comes out sunny-side up, and that is where we begin to put cracks in our foundation. By placing the struggle in our genetics (foundation), we chip away at our ability to see our fullest potential. It is easy to play victim to our genetics. Rather than resolving to find any means possible to live our purpose, we hide behind blood tests and stories passed on to us because it feels easier. Why would you put up a fight when generations have repeatedly waged the same war and lost? We lose such confidence in ourselves that we buy into the fallacy that "this is the way."

You might be sitting on your couch right now, all 5'3" of you and think, "Really? I could play basketball? I'm just hiding behind my genes? Wake up, Kirsten." Honestly, yes. Have you ever heard of Muggsy Bogues? He played for the Bullets, Hornets, Warriors, and Raptors. And there are 24 other NBA players that are under 5'9". Speaking of 5'9", that is also the height of the tallest female Olympic gymnast, Marie-Sophie Hindermann. I could run through countless sports analogies to prove to you that height is just a number. Genetics teach us that not everything is determined by nature. Environment (nurture) also plays a role in how we develop and grow.

Take a University of Minnesota research study1 that examined IQs of identical twins who were raised in the same environment versus identical twins who were raised separately. The results yielded enough difference for the researchers to conclude that there was a greater variance in IQ between identical twins who were raised apart than those who grew up in the same environment.

This is where I return to your genetic architecture. In what ways has your foundation incurred cracks? Are you buying into the storyline that you are too weak, fat, dumb, lazy, unworthy to see true transformation? Did you merely copy your family's house without question and hide yourself from the truth? Because the truth is that the foundation is set, but no one said you couldn't build a different house. That is your choice. The real struggle is in having the patience to build the home (Mind & Body). It is easy to start listening to your neighbors feeding you with their personal input on the "right" way to build, but it takes time and patience. Selecting the right building materials is challenging and time-consuming. If you build your mindset and body brick by brick and pick durable construction materials, you can weather any storm. Your siding might blow off or your windows might shatter, but the bones are so strong that you can always rebuild. Honestly, sometimes the storm rips the roof off because we need a rebuild. It's not a bad thing.

I have alluded to illness in many of these pages and dropped the genetic marker BRCA1 in this chapter because there is a part of my genetic story that I allowed to convince me that I would likely die prematurely and never have a legacy to leave behind, let alone pass on to a future child. Cancer runs through my family, as do heart disease and mental health struggles. After my father died, I walked in fear almost daily that I too would die, or worse, lose my mother. I never fully considered my own mortality. The letter revealing my positive testing for BRCA1 included positive test results for cancer. On that piece of paper, I saw a hopelessness in my genetics like I have never known. I had the tools and treatments necessary to manage my cancer, but I watched others, some far worse than myself and others far better (in my eyes), lose their battle. I sat in guilt and shame. I watched my mother care for a family friend dying from cancer and thought I was overreacting to my experience. I have spoken to friends, students, and strangers who have often felt this same "imposter syndrome" when they share their story. Many are afraid that because they didn't fit the Lifetime movie network version of a cancer patient, their struggle was somehow less traumatic and even less worthy of sharing. I have had students who shared their stories of successful surgeries, small rounds of radiation, and even chemotherapy treatments, but refused to identify as a survivor because the label felt alien to them. The stories they had heard didn't fit their experience.

I share this because every story matters, every struggle matters. And you may look at your genetics and think you are a "lucky one," or you may shake your fists and think that you are "cursed," but the story doesn't end there. The story doesn't stop with your struggle. It stops when you allow others to belittle your experience and tell you that your struggle is "less than."

You choose how to build your house. And you need to protect it. The former Under Armor campaign, "Protect This House," was a mantra I had on repeat on my MP3 player. That was a device some would listen to music on after Walkmans and CD players went out of fashion. (Remember those days?) If you want to protect your house, then choose wisely how you construct it. If you build it up with lies about your genetics defining who you are and what you are capable of, you will never fully experience the beauty of your architecture.

The possibilities for the construction of your home are entirely up to you. There are no limitations in your genetics, only insights on the direction in which you need to seek building materials. How will you build your house?

Chapter 10

UNDER THE INFLUENCE

"Keep taking time for yourself until you are you again."

—LALAH DELIA

STRUGGLES WILL NEVER BE A CHALLENGE TO FIND IN YOUR LIFE, especially if you have been hit at a particularly low point in your day, week, or even year. But how many of our struggles are the result of being *under the influence?* I am not talking about drugs or alcohol, although the particular "influence" to which I refer has become the most dangerous drug of this generation.

In today's times, we live for the high that comes from "likes," "shares," and "followers." We amass around people of interest solely based on the numbers in their social media profile as a justification for overtly obsessed behaviors of complete strangers (e.g. if you were "obsessed" with a person who had two followers, which were you and said person's mother, you would likely get serious backlash for such a foolish "follow.")

What is it about "influence" that has us altering our bodies, quitting our jobs, and abandoning our values in exchange for a few extra "hearts" from complete strangers who surely will not be at your side when real struggle appears at your door?

We all succumb to its allure; I am not immune. I find myself following teachers, celebrities, coaches, athletes, brands that have thousands and millions of followers, and feel somehow that by being one of the "followers," I am "in the know." That's part of it: We want to feel included, and if twenty million people are following Prince Harry, it cannot possibly be wrong to make yourself follower number twenty-million-and-one.

Let's rewind to the etymology of the word itself. The Latin word "*influentem*," "flowing in," is the root of the Old French "*influence*," which described that power was believed to flow from the stars. So influence permeates our thoughts, in a manner of speaking.

The "insta" world, which lives in abbreviated acronyms and sixty-second clips, makes it clear that simplifying concepts, ideas, and humans has become the new norm. How do we battle this new way of "connecting?" I use that word, "connecting," loosely because the intention of social platforms has long left where we are at in this point in time. *Influence is our currency—and people are dying for it.* Lives are lost because the comparisons and snapshots are too much to handle. Playing off our greatest fears of being alone and completely disconnected, we cave to the power of—influence.

ABSTINENCE

Have you ever taken a break from social media and noticed a positive change in your attitude, presence, and happiness? And yet, despite that, soon enough you come crawling back to the platforms?

Our addiction to these platforms gives light to the struggle we have in relationships, and why we see a higher rate of suicide and divorce. Bullying becomes a twenty-four-hours-a-day, three-hundred-sixty-five-days-a-year fight. Struggle multiplies in ways even struggle didn't know was possible. Do you have any idea how difficult it is to exceed the growth potential of struggle?

But what is the solution, because telling anyone to just "stop using the platforms" is about as effective as the health talk I received in seventh grade, when my teacher told the class that abstinence is the only answer to healthy relationships, unwanted pregnancies, and STDs.

BALANCE

I took a good look at how I was engaging in social media. I discovered being present as a result, and became aware of how my mood and health was changing due to my engagement. *The struggle of influence will continue to be one we battle, but awareness plays a role in how we engage its power.*

Influence does not have to be all bad: We can influence someone *for the better*, just as we can influence them to buy a product or idea. Influence can become a platform to change mindsets, education, and the world around us.

The struggle lies in the balance of the observer.

How do you sort through all the influence and determine which is authentic, and which is materialistically motivated? It requires turning back to your compass (Chapter 3).

You can only assess the other party's power and truth by holding your compass to its direction. If it pulls you away from your true north, your deepest sense of self, or compromises your beliefs, it is probably nothing more than a superficial influence that will wear off quickly. Its buzz will distort your ability to see clearly and send you a small degree off track, as it's hard not to get swept away by this. Your heart wants to believe that this person you have chosen to trust with your viewership and attention is looking out for you. But it's not always the case.

LEADERSHIP MARKERS

When you find someone whose influence has true power, you will see certain commonalities.

True leaders with influence give when they don't have to. They don't post about every donation or every hour they volunteer.

They care for others. Not because it helps them gain power, but because they are driven to leave the world a better place than they found it.

They grow continuously. Driven to never stop learning, these leaders love to challenge the way they think.

They live authentically. They don't speak love and compassion on the yoga mat, and then cut you off or tear down the cashier when the line is long. Who they are is transparent. They are not without flaw, but they don't try to hide the imperfection. They shine a light on the ways in which they are human.

They empower others. They are not fearful that sharing their knowledge or truth will rob them of their place in this world or the success they will achieve. Elevating those around them is just as much a part of their journey as the leadership they have acquired.

They manage hardship. They have bad days and feel overwhelmed like the rest of us. But they let hardship create opportunity for growth. They don't linger in the darkness when offered a light.

They serve with humility. They are humbled at the possibility that serving others has such a powerful reach. But they also rec-ognize that this power exists within every human being; it's just untapped potential in some.

These markers can help align your compass and evaluate how influence impacts your life.

As you begin to harness the power of your Struggle mas-tery, you will become a leader and influence others. People will be drawn to your story. Re-read these pages and remind your-self *how you can harness that influence for positive change.*

Influence is all around us. Change the narrative on how you harness its power and let its power impact you.

Chapter 11

SWIPE RIGHT, DODGE LEFT, STUCK CENTER

"Truth is, I'll never know all there is to know about you just as you will never know all there is to know about me. Humans are by nature too complicated to be understood fully. So we can choose either to approach our fellow human beings with suspicion or to approach them with an open mind, a dash of optimism and a great deal of candor."

—TOM HANKS

HUMAN BEINGS ARE COMPLICATED, COMPLEX ORGANISMS THAT cannot be fully categorized, labeled, or influenced. But there are plenty of ways in which we try to do all of the above when it comes to relationships. Just as easily as we can like and follow someone on social media, we can swipe, like, or remove potential partners. There are apps that allow us to swipe right if we are potentially interested in a person, and swipe left if we are not. *Why then do we always feel so stuck in the middle—static in our ability to connect with another human being?*

Growing up, I was conditioned by society to believe that you: go to school, graduate from college, get married, and have two kids and a pet of choice. While order often brings a sense of security, this linear progression of life as proposed by some unspoken scholar or patriarch also seems a little… dated. It's no wonder that we feel derailed if our plans are thwarted by struggle at any point on this train track set for us.

As an adult, I can now look back at relationships that I "missed out on," and see with a little better vision what hot messes I avoided, and what hurricanes I survived. I realize now that the relationships I valued in my youth are the ones that take up the least amount of memory. The damaged, messy relationships that still matter to me today have nothing to do with the eleventh-grade boy who rejected my professed love. Family, close friends, and even social relationships are the reels that keep playing in my mind.

Still, I sit and listen to some of my closest friends long for their true love and fail to give priority to the shattered relationship with their parents or siblings. I think secretly we all take for granted that our family will always "be there." It doesn't matter how dysfunctional the family, there is a part of us that lets the relationship just drift and bob in the harbor.

I lost my father before I was eight years old, and to this day it pains me to think of "what might have been" at times. But what goes deeper than the loss of my father were the ways I let pain and depression wedge a knife between my mother and me.

I was the kid who always believed life was rosier and greener everywhere else. I clung to the "traditional" families of friends of mine because I wanted to feel "normal." I hated being different, and not having my father at the dance. I hated having to find replacements in the moments that society said were designed "for fathers only."

And because my pain had stolen my words, I would let my actions of passive neglect to my family fill in the gaps.

By college, my relationship with my mother was better, but I knew she deserved more. I could blame her for not opening the door more, and diving deeper into the hurt I was feeling, but I know that even if she had, I wouldn't have been able to hear it. In this formative period of my life, I was discovering what many people in their teens learn about: love. And like I shared in my "bad case of authenticity" (Chapter 5), discovering my sexual orientation would most certainly drive a deeper wedge between those I love and me.

When I got engaged to my now wife, some of the people I cared for the most stopped talking to me. It wasn't just about my sexual orientation; I know that now. But at the time I felt betrayed, and I couldn't see how the web of lies I had spun to conceal the pain and anguish of my sexuality had impacted *their* lives.

WEDGE

When the people I loved turned their backs on me, I spent lonely nights in my apartment praying for death because I believed it would feel better than losing them.

I would try to reach out to them, but be completely denied. I would try to make amends, but instead got unanswered calls.

I am, and I was, no saint, not by any stretch of the imagination. But the loneliness, in some ways self-imposed, felt like too much to bear. Struggle was the only companion I could rely on—and it was not good at warm, fuzzy bedtime stories. It left me raw and challenged my willingness to change.

If it hadn't been for my partner, I may have lost hope forever. She wasn't scared by the dark clouds over me, or the lightning bolts of emotions that I felt. She greeted me with love and kindness, never wavering in her love. Her love moved through me and began to seal the gaping wounds of my failed relationships.

I saw her resolve to never let me give up on healing my relationship with my family and friends. After nearly three years of work, I mended the relationships that mattered most to me and learned to let go of the one's there weren't meant to be.

A TWO-WAY STREET

Relationship struggles are complex, because human beings are not fully predictable. And there are times where we want to cling to a relationship that is poisoning our very being, but we cannot let go. Fear takes hold of us and convinces us that by releasing this battered relationship, we could be left adrift at sea alone, and without hope of anyone searching for us.

I have seen this, as tattered relationships beat down the spirit of family members, students, teachers, mentors, and friends of mine. I have watched passively the burden of others carrying pain that was never theirs, and suffering the way my mother did when I shut down.

But a relationship is a two-way street, *and you can only control the side of the street in which you reside.* Owning your side of the story doesn't mean you have to stay in the relationship, and it certainly doesn't mean you have to settle. But it does come with a *deeply challenging struggle over making peace with the fact that you may not receive the answers or responses you want once you make your choice.*

True growth has come from examining the relationships that have failed me and hurt the most. They have given me the most honest lens through which to look at myself. I can see the ways I have bent to other people's will and caved in on my own morals. I can see those who are unworthy of my love and time, and therefore draw clearer boundaries going forward, so that I can reduce the likelihood of engaging in a relationship like that again.

RESHUFFLE

Take a long, hard look at who you surround yourself with most consistently—the top five people with whom you spend the most time. If you don't like the people who appear in your "top five," you might want to reshuffle the deck: *You begin to emulate the people with whom you surround yourself the most.*

As I have progressed in my relationship with struggle, I realize how present I must be in order to prioritize who is in my deck. I have reshuffled my deck countless times and even discarded some jokers. It's more than swiping left or unfriending someone. It's a consistent practice in awareness. If you notice your behaviors changing in a way that drives you further into struggle or a struggle mentality, take a look at your deck.

If you do this, there will be moments when you feel outnumbered; when it feels like you are all alone and there isn't a single person out there worthy of your time. *How long are you willing to wait for the people who are really meant to be in your inner circle?*

Grow your circle. Carefully.

Surround yourself with people who elevate your way of thinking.

Learn from teachers who push your edge.

Study from scholars who challenge the way you see the world.

These are the relationships that matter the most and build the foundations for the love of your life.

YOU

This brings me to the relationship I have been alluding to throughout this book: the relationship between you and you.

What is your relationship with yourself? Is it one that is positive? Or is it abusive and neglectful?

It's okay to be honest. I wish that you would be completely honest, not for my sake, but for the sake of your self-mastery.

Many days I have woken up, looked in the mirror, and convinced myself that I like what I see—but then gone on to subconsciously criticize every choice I made that day. My criticisms were the residue thoughts of past failed relationships, and people who didn't like me. (I know it's hard to believe that there are people that don't like me, but it's true.) Their criticisms were like seeds, and my self-inflicted insecurities and anxiety acted like fertilizer and water to them. The seeds grew slowly over time until I woke up one day and didn't even recognize the face in the mirror. Suddenly, I saw the face of what *everyone else* said I would be.

Maybe it's time to go back to the mirror and erase all the criticisms. Use a little Windex, because the remnants of fault-finding are sticky.

When I apply the Windex, I can take a good look at the person who is really staring back—and realize she is more brilliant than I remember.

UNBURDEN

Seeing myself for the first time, I can feel a weight being lifted from my shoulders. I begin to realize that the negative relationships, doubters, and naysayers have piled on masks that tried to keep me from seeing the power and beauty that has existed within me all along.

I spend more time trusting myself and my instincts. The questions that used to unravel my thoughts expand my observation of the ways in which I have carried the burden of past failed relationships for too long.

Refusing to shoulder another person's burdens reveals the magnitude of relationships. The smallest of interactions may cling to your personal perceptions of yourself like a piece of clothing without a Bounce sheet.

Unsticking those thoughts begins with an honest look at who you are, and who you want to be.

Chapter 12

HUMBLE PIE IS
MAKING ME FAT

"Let me remind you: wherever your focus is directed
that's where your energy goes. Whatever you allow
in your space, you will eventually become."

—UNKNOWN

"BE RESPECTFUL."

"Don't talk back."

"If you don't have anything nice to say, don't say anything at all."

These lies manifest into rolls on my body I didn't even see adding up.

Walking through the mall, I would venture over into the men's section of each clothing store pretending that I was shopping for my son, husband, dad, boss—who knows? Then, carrying an armful of men's clothing I hoped would fit my, um, larger body, I would also grab a couple of women's items to throw off the dressing room attendant so I could make it look like I was just there to try on the women's clothing in my hands.

Every now and again, an attendant would say, "Oh, I can hold onto those [the men's clothes] out here for you if you would like, so you don't have to carry them."

Considering I would just hang them up on a hook in the fitting room, this logic never made much sense to me. But if I acquiesced, then I would have to pretend like none of the women's clothes ended up fitting, only to have to take the men's clothes home to try on, and return later what didn't fit me.

Not only is this costly and not very efficient, but many times I ended up being too lazy to even return the stuff that didn't fit.

"I'm sure I'll get fit enough to make this top work at some point, so I'll just hold on to it."

The excuses I had to justify a laundry list of self-denial about my weight is pretty terrifying when I look back at it.

To make it less obvious to others that I had bought a men's shirt, I tried to keep the colors as "feminine" as possible, with oranges and pinks. Plus, I stuck to plain shirts with no writing on them for a little more camouflage.

I was secretly outing myself in these clothes. So not only was I heavy; I was also screaming from the closet, Look at me, *I'm clearly a lesbian!*

RECOGNITION

A reckoning was just around the corner for me, though. In the bridesmaid section of a David's Bridal, I heard five words that shook me to my core:

"We don't carry Plus Sizes."

Wait, what? PLUS? I've never been a plus size in my life! All my shirts say "medium!"

Sure, they are men's shirts, and most of them run large, but they are **mediums**.

How did I get to this point? What life experiences had derailed me so much that I didn't even recognize the body in the full-length mirror in front of me?

The tears rolled down my cheek as I sat in a dressing room trying to muffle the sobs over the embarrassment of what I had become. I ended up having to search all over the web for stores that carry larger sizes for the bridesmaid dress I needed for my friend's wedding.

PAPER CUTS

Like many of you, I was conditioned by this world to think that there must be a *single* trauma that leads me off the path instead of a thousand little paper cuts that finally cause me to bleed out. I was ashamed that there wasn't anything overtly awful over the course of my life up to this point that could justify this foreign shadow I could not detach from, much less hide from.

Humble pie was making me fat. I stuffed down the thoughts of frustration or going off the deep end to speak my mind because I was taught repeatedly to "hold my tongue" and "be respectful." And yet the tongue lashings from people around me— not strangers but "friends" and "peers"—cut through me like a knife. The potential employers who had told me as a woman I wasn't qualified, or that because I was gay I couldn't be good enough, built up this layer around me that I thought was a protective shield, but it was really a "fatty barrier" between me and what I was feeling.

I now get why there are "break rooms" where people smash and shatter items to release the pent-up rage that has remained buried deep within them.

Is it possible that some moments require a voice… dare I write, a ROAR?

MAKE NICE

Walking on eggshells at well over two hundred plus pounds is really a joke; I walk about as delicately as Godzilla through the city.

I want to blame the world for telling me that, as a woman, if I use my voice, I am a "bitch," or if I speak my mind, I'm "unstable." *I am tired of holding my breath*, afraid that what I have to say might ruffle some feathers or make me unpopular.

I'm not advocating a full outrage storm at your boss as you put in your notice, but I am saying that *RESPECTFULLY telling someone they can "shove" it just might be necessary if we ever want to see change.*

I have gone on hikes before, and stood at the top of mountains, and shouted my battle cry, and have had imaginary conversations with the person or business that I am at odds with, *just to feel as though the words have been said.* A therapist pointed out to me once—which really only made me angrier in some ways—that I let the fear of being unpopular for speaking the truth, respectfully, keep me from freeing myself of this heaviness I am not meant to carry.

Why is it that they who slice-and-dice get to walk away scot-free and weightless? While I carry the twenty pounds of their shit in my mind and body for twenty-plus years? This goes on even though I can quote the best philosophers and eastern monks of this time who say that I (we) have given them the power, and that no one has the ability to make me (us) angry or feel unjust without my (our) permission.

But it seems that in kindergarten, after learning my letters,

I signed a life permission slip allowing anyone I encounter to hurt me and cause me pain without me protesting vociferously.

ROAR

I've had it up to *here* with trying to "make nice" and win other people's favor. I pile on the extra shifts, work the extra holidays, take the pay cut. That horoscope from so long ago that promised "respect" deceived me, and I have created a path where respect seems to be something that eludes me. People love to exploit my generosity and heart for service—*and I mistook it for respect.*

I settle in this darkness of defeat, and then wander out like a lion from its den with a roar so loud I wonder, *Why can no one hear me?* I remember sitting on a mountain looking out... actually, that's a lie. I was sitting in my car at the twentieth red light, wondering, *How did you get here? Who ARE you?*

My surface-level self was quick to respond, *You are a child of God, a lover of life...*

I'm gonna stop myself there; I was a walking Hallmark card and Instagram bio.

Who am I? was already in the question itself: *I AM*—the present tense of "to be."

I am being. I am the present. I am the living. I am the breath. I am the anger. I am the love. I am the light. I am the darkness. I am all that is, in this moment.

And in this moment—I am a woman who is out of shape, depressed, alone, and cut off from herself. I stopped being "I am" because I could only linger in the "I was" and the "I was not." Screeched to a halt because I only looked from a lens of my past trying to conceal the pain of my present.

I'm tired of bearing weight that was never mine to carry. I am not Atlas, and I have not been entrusted with the world. So maybe it's time I took the globe off my shoulders and started looking at what it means to know, *"I am."*

One thing I know for sure: "I am" is tired of letting Humble Pie make her fat. The uncertainty now resides in what will lead to true happiness and connection to the great "I am" within me.

Now it's time, guru, to ask yourself what is holding you back. In what ways has your voice felt silenced? Is there a way in which you can release the weight of other people's influence and pressure, and free yourself to fully "BE"?

Chapter 13

RUNNER'S HIGH

"I get addicted to the feelings associated with the end of a long run."

—KRISTIN ARMSTRONG

EVERYONE IS CHASING "THE HIGH." FOR SOME, IT COMES FROM A more acceptable vice, like running or exercise, extreme sports, or breathtaking adventures. But even "high" has its limits, and the pursuit can be as deadly as its side effects.

I can recall my mother asking me why I ran. She would recount how miserable and anxious I looked before running, during running, and even just after completion. "If you are always so miserable, why do you do it?" she would then ask.

A conditioned response from a lifetime of fitness and sports advertising would fall from my lips: "The runner's high."

Truth be told, I had no idea growing up what that phrase meant, but everyone made it sound so great that I just rolled with it. Some described it as an "euphoric" feeling you get after the run. Others more scientifically explained the hormonal rise of serotonin to the brain, exciting the pleasure center of our thoughts. Still others recounted it as an overwhelming joy that directly correlated with their accomplishment.

As I wasn't experiencing such sensations after running, I thought that I was running wrong. *Maybe it is only activated when you run at a certain speed or distance*, I reflected.

Soon I became so obsessed with chasing the elusive "runner's high" that I forgot to be present in the experience itself. *Forget what was happening in the beginning and middle; let's get right to the end where you feel the high.*

ACCEPTABLE "FIXES"

Interestingly enough, society applauds and embraces those whose high comes from such athletic "struggles." But for less socially acceptable addictions—like drugs or alcohol—society becomes both judge and jury. Addiction gets ranked, for example. *Smoke marijuana, and you are lazy and leeching off society. Smoke cigarettes, and let me get you a covered prescription for the patch that will help you overcome it. Become addicted to painkillers, get written off. Become addicted to sugar, have some insulin.*

All of these perspectives are about what really comes down to what we, as a society, deem "acceptable." Very few calls are made for an intervention for someone addicted to extreme exercise programs, but talk about your addiction to pornography and people want to lock you up. *We cannot condemn one person and console the other—yet we do this all the time.*

If your addiction can be classified as something a middle- or upper-class white person is struggling with, then we can find a way to overcome. If your addiction is tied to being a lower-class minority individual, you have done this to yourself and you deserve the consequences.

Beware of smoke and mirrors in the wellness and fitness industry, because you can trade your "societal Scarlet letter addiction" for a more suitable and acceptable one. ("Act now and we will throw in a T-shirt, shaker bottle, and a private social media group full of others with the same addiction to tell you how awesome you are.")

Are you starting to see that there is more connection to the "runner's high" and cocaine addicts than you ever realized? Addiction is a condition of dependency, craving, habit. Talk to a "gym rat" about a rest day, and they will be itching to get their gym fix as much as a drug addict is searching for their next score. Sugar addicts fly under the radar as long as their waistline is in check. But if their scales start tipping closer to Shamu the killer whale—like I felt mine were—they will have judgment passed on them as fast as they can walk past someone.

ROCK STAR

I have spent my life exchanging one addiction for another, more socially acceptable one. And while I have never done drugs or been addicted to alcohol, I have been addicted to more food, people, experiences, and places because each gave me a "high" that made me feel connected to something bigger than myself. Yet the high was just a means to reach something greater than my human existence. ***The core of the high I sought out was to elevate myself.***

I wanted that brief moment of feeling like I just high-fived God and came back to earth—a total rock star.

The cycle of addiction isn't just about the high. It's about the glimmer of greatness we feel in that moment, to which we want to return again and again. Struggle is where I have grown—where the high became more than a flickering glitter bomb bursting in the moment. ***Struggle is the edge which skating upon opens more than my eyes: It exposes my thoughts and spirit.***

I stopped chasing the moments of greatness when I stood with struggle and humbled myself to its lessons.

As a coach, I use different metric ratings for my athletes' efforts. Some are more objective and scientific than others. But RPE, or rate of perceived exertion, has been my most telling. The scale is one to ten. One is when I am at complete ease. Ten is when I am dying and could not give one more ounce of energy.

Take two athletes with similar builds, strength, endurance, and VO2 max (maximal oxygen consumption). I can give them the same workout and get vastly different data on its difficulty. Athlete 1 may rate it a five, and say that it wasn't awful but it wasn't great. Athlete 2 may tell me it's a nine, and they nearly saw Jesus in the process. Why would two athletes with such similar physical and athletic make-up have such vastly different RPEs? There are many scientific theories, but my experiences of more than two decades have shown that the differentiating factor is—STRUGGLE.

Disclaimer: What follows is a completely subjective hypothesis and conclusion based only on my experiences over the years in exercise science, physical education, strength and conditioning, and all other forms of fitness I have studied.

The struggle factor has shaped how I successfully help athletes navigate their training. This "struggle factor" breaks down into three categories: Personal, Educational, Technical—P.E.T. for short. Examining each athlete's P.E.T.s gives a clearer picture of the training methods that will help them reach success. *Personal* examines Maslow's hierarchy of needs. Often portrayed in the shape of a pyramid, the largest, most fundamental needs reside at the bottom, and the need for self-actualization and transcendence sits at the top. The crux of the theory is that an individual's most basic needs must be met before they become motivated to achieve higher levels of needs. Asking questions to unravel this "personal" section of the athlete history is just the beginning.

Education isn't just a matter of how much knowledge they have acquired or which degrees they have earned. This tool is about how they learn. Are they visual, auditory, reading/writing, or kinesthetic? Then I will inquire about their higher education experiences.

Finally, I look at the *technical* skills of the sport or goal they are working towards. I evaluate their understanding and proficiency in these skills, and then build a program based on the gap between skills they excel at and skills they are deficient in.

The acronym P.E.T. is by design. A pet is a tamed animal kept for companionship. It builds a stronger relationship with struggle. Here I go again with a shift in perception. So much of my ability to become my own Struggle Guru has been about reworking the angle at which I see the problem.

Athletes who take their struggles and really start to work into the problem mold a new object out of the mud they have been handed. They step back and find another angle to approach their struggle and meet the challenge where it is at, rather than try and just attack it.

The athletes that are shifting their perspective on struggle are also the athletes who have known true, deeply challenging struggle. They are willing to push harder and perceive the challenges as less difficult than those who have had less experience with struggle. This does not mean that both athletes will not grow to be world-class in their sport. However, their perception of struggle does play a crucial role in how they train.

Yet, as I watch the world of sports, fitness, and wellness search for any little nugget of an edge to be had, it becomes clear to me that struggle is one that not many even *attempt* to pick up! Struggle merely gets lumped into inspiration and drive and sports psychology mindset training.

When was the last time a coach and teacher dove into what struggles you were dealing with in your day-to-day life, and/or plunged deeply into the struggles that have made you the person you are today? For the normal day-to-day teacher, doing so would be overwhelming and exhausting. The ratio between students and teachers alone creates a challenge. The overwhelming amount of information to discuss with each student would prove to be time consuming and not very practical. But if you are working one-on-one with a coach, they *should* be asking these important questions.

Even if your sport of choice is LIFE.

THE SPORT THAT IS LIFE

Life is a knockout, kick-butt, endurance race wrapped into a rock-climbing cliff-dive kind of sport. Struggle is perhaps most relevant for these types of "athletes." Coaches reading this book should consider how they can develop training plans that go beyond periodization, nutrition, sleep, and mindset training, and look at developing programs where struggle is the load in which your athletes bear to stretch and grow.

Struggle is our greatest teacher.

You pause and say, "No, *failure* is the greatest teacher."

Failure is a part of struggle. When you struggle, failure is a part of the equation. **But not every failure comes out of a struggle. Sometimes failure happens because we didn't prioritize. That test you didn't prepare for, not because the subject was too hard, but** *because hanging out with friends was a bigger priority at the time. That's not a "struggle"; that's lack of preparedness.*

Don't let the hype about failure make you blind to your coach or teacher. Read autobiographies and memoirs of some of the world's greatest athletes, teachers, philosophers, scientists, doctors, and researchers. Their stories include failure, *but it is the STRUGGLE that helped shape them into the greatest minds and athletes the world has known.* Struggle built their perseverance. Perseverance blossomed into discipline, and discipline is just the official name and title "freedom" resides under.

By leaning into struggle, you will find freedom. Freedom in mind, body, spirit. No single person can give you those gifts. God instills within each of us the divine tools to explore the gifts and power of being.

But He also gave free will. He set us up to make a conscious choice to explore that which was freely given.

PARADOX

For quite some time I let "the high" become my guru. Shamelessly, I followed fitness fad after fitness fad. I thought I could eat, train, and inspirationally quote "the way" for me.

But I came to realize it was more than that. Just like that, with the snap of a finger, I could see my struggle—as my teacher. And if you believe that, I have some oceanfront property in the Sahara I'd love to sell you as well.

So the everyday reality is, I can see glimmers of self-mastery in my struggle at times. But then I also experience equal parts madness and depression. If landing on my yoga mat has taught me anything, it's that every day is different. I cannot become so attached to the "mastery" that I miss being present in the moment offering it.

Confused yet?

"Which is it, Kirsten? Should I become the guru of struggle in my life, or be present with the struggle and unattached to it?"

Both! This is the paradox of life. ***Embrace the moment, in the moment that you feel masterful, but also humbly accept that you are both the master AND the student. Never are you just one. You will always be both.***

This concept is freeing for me. When I *feel*, I view through the eyes of the student. When I experience *the moment of mastery*, I humbly bow as the teacher.

Do not confuse the student with a scapegoat for blame, like with genetics (Chapter 9). Instead, *see the vulnerability that comes with being a student, and recognize that the mis-step is a stepping stone to understanding your limitations.* From this understanding, you can seek out experiences and teachings that draw you closer to—mastery.

Remember, it will *always* be a balancing act. This is why "chasing the high" is not sustainable or practical. You will forever be caught in a race to reach the next summit, and fulfillment will become shallow and fleeting with your age and abilities. Your authentic self will continue to be covered by the mass of influence and opinion around you, and the finish line will continue to be moved.

Your search for understanding will open you to other students around you who seek the wisdom you have acquired. Do not begrudgingly withhold your knowledge in fear of their advancement. *Freely sharing your wisdom will help develop the guru within both of you.*

Chapter 14

PULL UP A CHAIR

*"Chair pose is the defiance of spirit, showing how high
you can reach even when you are forced down."*

—UNKNOWN

AS A YOGA TEACHER, I REALIZE THAT AS SOON AS I INSTRUCT THE
class to take certain poses, everyone cringes a little. The faces
around the room immediately look like I put a lemon in their
mouth and told them to suck it. *Too real? It's the truth.*

Chair pose is one of those movements that is a real lemon
biter, a seemingly simple posture that is chock-full of complexity. Using a soft, compassionate voice, I try to seduce my
students into believing it's merely about squeezing their thighs
together as they sit down and throw their arms up like glitter
at a pride parade. But this pose feels nothing like sitting down
in a chair—and often has their baby-deer legs shaking from
the first breath in and a small inferno quickly building in their
upper back.

Yet the pose is also one of the most telling postures for my students. *The struggle in this pose is known by all who have chosen to land on their mat.* And what comes next is why I love teaching so much: The breath deepens, and the class collectively sounds like Darth Vader as sweat droplets bead up on their skin.

At this point, I encourage everyone to "sink a little lower" —and receive a strong energy to my third eye that I might get hit if I ask them to go any deeper. Naturally, I shift from the depth of their seat to the length in which they will hold it. The struggle is building in their legs; their arms start to bend and look a little more like a cactus than lightning bolts of power reaching for the sky. Some will come out of the pose, whilst others stare around the room in a game of chicken with those surrounding their mat. All wait with bated breath for the moment of release.

I jokingly share, "I can't keep you here forever; the class is only sixty minutes." The joke lands with no one. Finally, I free them of the pose and guide them into a forward fold. We pause in quiet reflection of relief.

Reflection feels minimal when they realize for the last thirty seconds in chair pose, they held their breath and increased their heart rate so much that the only thing they want to do right now is drop to child's pose, a common pose often used as a resting position. There are moments as a teacher, I hope that by surrendering into child's pose they might deepen their breath and reflect on the fact that *something in the moment which felt like an insurmountable struggle was overcome by the power of their physical and mental strength.*

If struggle were a path of hot coals, stopping along each burning lump would be a sign of insanity, not strength. And yet, as a teacher, I am asking you to take up residency on the hot coals and make peace with it. The metaphor feels a bit forced—*we land on our mat to learn how to approach the life we live off the mat*. If you think it is impossible to stay in chair pose but do it, *your mind begins to fantasize about the other things in your life you thought you couldn't do, but actually can. You stretch the boundaries of the physical and mental body*.

Struggle will arise in life; the fire, wall, and crashing waves are unavoidable. And I have attended enough conferences, lectures, workshops, and classes that told me to learn how to navigate around struggle. The leaders of these workshops will talk of mastering "how to see struggle coming," but at the same time tell me to "be more present." Well, my yogi mind can't seem to wrap itself around all of the future tenses of these methods. *Which is it? Be present or look to the future? It's the same conundrum that comes with chair pose: Which is it, sit down or reach up?* Doing both simultaneously feels impossible.

DROP DOWN, RISE UP

It was while I was sitting in chair pose at a small studio in Akron, Ohio, where the teacher thought that two minutes was not a long enough hold in chair pose, that something clicked, or maybe snapped. It was hard to tell because everything was burning, and I swore I was dying. I might even have blacked out for part of the experience. But what I know is that after that class, another struggle was waiting at the studio exit. This one was bigger than before; it was one that pushed the boundaries of my sanity and threatened my virtues.

I thought to myself, *What the hell? I'm just trying to elevate myself, and here is struggle trying to rip me down*. And so... I laughed. I mean, *crazy woman laughing in a crowd with everyone questioning my sanity; it was really loud laughing!* I was laughing because after

I thought that statement, I saw a chair randomly sitting in the parking lot on the grass right near the curb. *A chair!*

That was the first time I saw my yoga practice as more than physical activity. I realized that when my teacher asked me to drop into chair, she wasn't talking about dropping into a squat. She was asking me to *drop into the feelings, sensations, and shit holding me down while simultaneously asking me to be my own hero and rise up. She was encouraging me to sit with the past that might tell me, "I cannot," but bring the breath of this present moment into the now.*

It wasn't about calculating the struggle of being in chair pose by comparing past holds in the posture. It wasn't about distracting my thoughts in the now and forgetting the past. Allowing the thoughts from past chair holds to arise, bubble up, and make me want to get out of the pose was the struggle. Releasing those thoughts through powered breath is how the present built new pathways for me to travel in the future.

I could finally see that past, present, and future are rooted in the same mindset.

WEED WHACK

I don't sit in classes and actively dissect every pose, wondering about its profound life lesson. But I *do* stay in the moment to feel every pose, breath, and droplet of sweat. My body is the student. My mind, the teacher. My breath, the guru. Each time I land on my mat, I bring the struggles that have filled the vessel of my body and mind, and ask my breath to lead the way in educating both.

Observation of my mind and body over more than a decade of physical practice has left my thoughts—all over the map. Some days I may only be able to stay present in what my body is feeling. Another practice may reveal the waves of thoughts crashing through my mind. There are a few moments, which have increased in frequency over time, where I can make the connection between a physical practice and explore its lesson off the mat. It's why I feel defensive at times over the sales pitch that there is "just one key" necessary for any one of us to emulate and presto, no more "struggle bus."

As you read this chapter, check in with the feelings that arise. *Did she just ask me to check my feelings? Sure did. Because the emotions are valid.* If reading this one tiny snapshot of one moment of clarity for me pisses you off, ask yourself, *Why?* It's making you angry for a reason. Don't avoid it. Lean into it. Maybe it's the fact that you haven't felt that, and you feel jaded that you have been busting your behind for so long to try and overcome struggle but are still sitting in the thick of it. Or you might be upset because the pressure of struggle has left you overwhelmed. You need to get seriously deep with how you are feeling.

Struggle has a best friend named Fear. They are like a WWE Super Duo that taps the other in as soon as you feel strong enough to conquer one. Before you know it, you are on a mat in the center ring just waiting to be tapped out.

You are the guru in your struggle. No one else can equally duplicate its power in you and over you. But if you think that one chapter, book, or person will be able to swoop in with the answer for you, then the struggle and feelings tied to it are going to grow.

Bust out the weed wacker. It's time to clear out the mental landscape of all the weeds that are overgrown and smothering your life.

Pull up a chair, because this might take a while.

GURU HOME PRACTICE: "PULL UP A CHAIR"

Today, this moment, I am going to advise you to do something that makes you sit in discomfort. It doesn't mean you physically have to hold a pose, but *get outside your comfort zone, then sit with how this discomfort and uneasiness makes you feel.* Spend two to three minutes writing down everything about your experience.

Chapter 15

TUNNEL VISION

"Your vision will become clear only when you can look into your own heart. Who looks outside, dreams; who looks inside, awakens."

—CARL JUNG

WE HAVE BEEN TOLD WE HAVE THE POWER TO CHANGE. BUT THE road that leads to this change tunnels right through our emotional nerve endings, and we shudder at the idea of even entering this tunnel. Strategically placed signs remind us to remove the rose-colored glasses before entering the tunnel to ensure our headlights are on.

I don't think I can be the only one who feels like her high beams are broken, and another headlight completely busted. Rather than fix this before entering the tunnel, most of us rely on others entering the same tunnel to provide us with enough light to get us through. Sure, this works, but when we get to the other side, we don't really have any new tools or growth from our time in the darkness. This is where we perpetually begin following, damn near riding, the asses of others ahead of us. We don't want to end up in another tunnel alone. We don't have the light to illuminate our path.

It's a visual to which we can relate, but one we hardly ever step back from to evaluate: Why are we always so keen on the light of others?

We follow because we *lack trust in ourselves and our skill sets*. And honestly, part of it is that we have been following other people's light so much, we might not have the understanding or know-how on how to train these skills. That's what I want to discuss: *Which of our skills are lacking in our getting-to-know-how-to-navigate-life memoirs?*

Be honest. Because for me, I realized I knew—very little. I lived in a fifteen-mile radius of where I grew up because I needed all the familiar light possible. I didn't risk in love. I played it safe right out of college and took a job I knew I would hate but which paid well. I blew my salary on a best friend and other lights to keep me away from the darkness. But when my world imploded before my eyes, I was trapped in the tunnel with zero light to guide me. It was here I made my first honest assessment of myself, and I recognized I really had very little skill for this moment. It was time to dive deep into my abilities, strengths, and weaknesses, and start developing "tunnel vision." *I needed focus so narrow, and that which is often called "selfish," to see who I was, and what I am capable of.* **I had to fail, cry, break down, kick, and scream to get to the core of who I am and honestly start changing.**

LIGHTS, CAMERA, ACTION

Changing is harder than making the list of strengths and weaknesses. It requires action. Anyone can write the words, but carrying them out is flippin' mortifying.

The tunnel vision began with owning my truth. And owning my truth meant writing what I really wanted and saying it out loud. It's more than speaking our truth to the universe, because if that is all it takes, then I would like to be independently wealthy and live in a treehouse near the ocean.

Nope, looks like it takes more than that.

The familiar struggles outlined in this book are more than reference points for you to connect to. Seeing that you are not alone in the struggle universe is a beginning, but not an action plan. Telling others about struggles you are experiencing and gathering resources is the research stage of your tunnel vision. But I want to know how you plan on *making it through* the tunnel. I need you to get through the tunnel with me.

I also am calling on you as a fellow Struggle Guru to empower others to be their own guru. Arming you with talking points that connect us will get people to the door, but it doesn't invite them to stay very long. It's time to put away the shades and wipe off your headlights because you are gonna high beam your way through the tunnel.

This is where you step out of the theory and move forward into your mastery. If these pages have shown you anything, it's that you have the skills and experience to navigate this path. Trust your gut. It doesn't get entangled in the emotions of your mind.

ILLUMINATE

Take a moment and reflect on the previous chapters: *Which chapter jumps out at you?* Don't overthink or analyze it. Go take that chapter and sit quietly, or find a place where you can walk and be with your thoughts. Run through the chapter in your mind and let the words, feelings, and experiences flow. If you are sitting quietly, you can set a timer for five minutes. If you are walking and want to walk for longer than that, you can, just place your phone on voice recorder and start talking it out. You can let the thoughts flow freely to help you work through this tunnel vision.

THROUGH THE TUNNEL MEDITATION

As you close your eyes, envision the chapter title you selected sitting at the end of the tunnel. Notice the length of the tunnel. Take in the shadows and light.

Are you the only one in the tunnel, or do you see anyone else? What thoughts or feelings arise as you think of the chapter you selected? How many different senses can you bring to this experience? Do you feel anything as you move through this tunnel? Are there particular surfaces you walk across?

Is there a breeze? What does the temperature feel like against your skin? Is there a familiar scent in the air as you walk? What subtle scents do you smell? Can you taste anything? What do you see?

Are there shapes, colors, people, things that you can make out as you walk closer to the end of the tunnel? As you move closer to the end, do you feel any differently than when you started?

Open your eyes.

Write down as much as you remember from this meditation. Don't worry about *how much* you remember; your mind is doing the heavy lifting by filtering out the pieces that are unnecessary.

NAVIGATING

Once you have completed the meditation exercise, it's time to make a plan. Look at your list and decide what action you can take based on this list. Divide your list into senses. Note which memories from your meditation correlate with sight, sound, smell, touch, and taste. This will help determine the means by which you can best navigate the tunnel you have chosen.

If, for example, your list is predominantly things you can see with your eyes and your chapter was labels (Chapter 8), I want you to think about all the labels people see when looking at you. Because your subconscious was drawn predominantly to things you see, your struggle in labels will have a stronger pull in terms of the visual labels you worry others might see. Look at, and write down, all the labels that could describe you based on visual appearance only. Do any of the labels make you feel uneasy or negative? Write down those labels. Then write down the labels that make you feel good, loved, and positive.

By separating the labels into positive and negative, you can now become deeply focused on how to master this struggle. When you look at the negative labels, who was it who gave you this label? Was it a person? A group? Society? Media? Then ask yourself how you feel about that person or group. For example, I see the word "homo" as derogatory. I had friends use that word in front of me before I came out. Even after I came out, I had some who responded to me with, "You're a homo?"

That label that I correlate negatively comes from people with whom I am no longer friends. So I can dismiss this label holding any power over me. *Note that not every label will be so easy to dismiss.*

Today that word doesn't upset me as it once did because I realized I couldn't just remove the label—a misconception I held for far too long. *I had to get to the root of who labeled me that way and how my relationship with those people needed to change.* In my case, I realized, after sitting down with them, that they were unwilling to change the verbiage even though they knew it hurt me. So in order to heal, I needed to remove the label and let go of their friendship.

The process of releasing the friendship and the label is not an easy task. It isn't as simple as saying, "Bad label, a bad person. They are cut off." But it can provide some insight on why you are hung up on some labels more than others. When the label is negative and comes from someone you love, like a parent or sibling, it becomes even more challenging. You might not feel ready to end that relationship. But you may need to set better boundaries for yourself so you can limit how much power that label holds over you.

This is *"tunnel visioning"*: *You work through a sensory meditation envisioning the problem at the end of the tunnel and let your mind soak in as much information as possible. Then you can sit down and take two minutes to write down everything you remember and sort the sensory memories.*

For such a seemingly silly meditation, tunnel visioning is one of my favorites in navigating struggle. Doing so begins to reveal a lot about how we receive information, process struggle, and grow. When I started this meditation style, I was teaching breast cancer patients post-mastectomy how to cope with struggle after surgery. For many of these women, it was the visual sensory memories they recalled the most. And through tunnel visioning, together we could work through physical body struggle and begin to process ways to change their mindset and view of themselves.

I have put aside a special journal that I use just for these tunnel vision meditations. I chose a journal that is colorful and bright, to remind me that struggle doesn't always have to be dark and serious. I make sure to include some of the lighter moments of my meditation in my journal as well. It's okay to laugh now and again at some of the funny shit our brain attaches itself to.

Remember that not every tool works for everyone: If you do this exercise a couple of times and it just feels wasteful, my feelings are not hurt. (*Okay, so maybe a little bit, because I have spent a long time developing this.*) It might not work for you, and that is okay. Do not beat yourself up and think that mastering struggle is hopeless. Tunnel vision simply provides another perspective of struggle, and we know that it takes seeing the struggle from multiple angles to really harness your inner guru.

Tuck the technique away for a rainy day when inevitably a friend or co-worker seeks your counsel, and share this method with them. The more gurus we add to the community, the deeper the pockets of tools begin to exist to help others.

Chapter 16

PATH OR BARRICADE

*"Choice is the most powerful tool we have. Everything boils
down to choice. We exist in a field of infinite possibilities.
Every choice we make shuts an infinite number of doors
and opens an infinite number of doors. At any point
we can change the direction of our lives by a simple choice.
It is all in our hands, our hearts, and our minds."*

—UNKNOWN

CALL ME CHILDISH, BUT BEATING THE GPS'S EXPECTED ARRIVAL TIME
is an extreme sport for me. There is something satisfying about
defying the voice that told you repeatedly that you will not
arrive at your destination for a set number of minutes or hours
and proving them wrong.

When someone sees us struggling and says, "Don't worry,
in another week you won't even blink at this struggle. You
will look back and laugh," we immediately want to beat the
arbitrarily created time constraint they proposed. We fixate on

the time element rather than the problem itself. This blissful ignorance of the power we personally possess to navigate this hardship appears, and a deeper, more learned person emerges; instead, we resist. Our brain scrambles to find shortcuts and hidden passageways. The internal GPS keeps trying to reroute us, but even the soft British accent we selected starts to sound boiling mad as we blatantly ignore her directions.

Struggle isn't what throws us off our path. Nope, you did that all by yourself. (*Tough to hear, but true.*) Struggle didn't tell you to bushwhack through the uncharted wilderness when there is a perfectly paved road ahead of you. You charted your own course and assumed that there would be some visible or audible sounds to assure you one way or another if you were on the correct path or needed to turn around.

Sure, an alarm goes off in our brains that initially alerts us of struggle. Usually, we don't even hear the buzzing of the first and instead wait until the second alarm goes off, "Abandon ship, we are sinking!"

(*There aren't enough lifeboats. I'll never let go. Wait, that last one was a scene from Titanic. Sorry about that.*)

Your mind panics in struggle because it's uncomfortable, and for many of us, these are uncharted waters. The water's chop and the precarious clouds above are unnerving. ***How will you become the captain of your own ship if every single time the weather turns sideways, you jump out and bail?*** You cannot possibly expect to master the high seas in the tiny lifeboat you are floating on, at the mercy of the ocean.

Let's not draw an extreme conclusion based on this understanding, though: I am not suggesting that you put yourself in struggle's path and "hunker down" to embrace the storm. Struggle will find you at the times you need its lessons most.

And even though it feels like struggle is trying to throw you overboard, I am merely suggesting that *when struggle's storms begin to brew, you pause for a moment and evaluate the skills you have to work through the storm.*

You don't have to *have* all the skills. You can recruit a crew. You can hire a teacher to help you become more proficient in navigation, or take lessons in how to sail. But please, please, try to stay the course. Learn to notice the subtle lessons of life. Don't be afraid as you mature and learn, to reroute when it is in the best interest of your growth and development. You might be asking, "When will I know it is?" If I were to respond, *In time you will become more instinctual,* you might throw this book in the air, and hurt the closest person near you. So I will elaborate.

ABANDON OR DIG IN

Time is a great teacher and cannot, will not, be rushed. If you choose to try to bypass time, it will only catch up to you and divert you to a longer path. Time does not like to be manipulated and unappreciated.

As you begin to evaluate all of the education and skills you have in struggle, you will see patterns. After all, history is doomed to repeat itself if we do not learn the lesson. If you can see patterns in personal relationships that have failed, look at whether or not you abandoned the ship too soon. Some of your answers may be more obvious than others. A person who is verbally tearing you down all the time is a valid reason to let go, abandon ship, of that relationship. Refusing to let go of your pride and apologize to someone you love because you would rather be right than lose the ego and grow your relationship is a sign of abandoning too soon.

Not all paths are black and white. Time will bring wisdom and help you discern when you need to abandon that ship or dig into the lessons of the storm. Time gifts you with more knowledge and education.

SHORTCUTS

Beating out the expected arrival time of the GPS doesn't outrun struggle. It lets struggle know that you are ready for the next challenge. Maybe slowing down in the struggle and learning a little more from the experience isn't such a bad thing.

You might think you have all the answers and want to jump to the end of the book. Yet the very key to mastering your struggle could reside in the few pages you skipped. Shortcuts might work when you are running late for work, but they don't work with struggle. Struggle has a path within its path within its path.

Don't be discouraged by this truth: It frees you of attachments to perfection in life. Life is bumpy, messy, gritty, and tough. You will learn lessons you thought you had mastered. You will rally around an idea or concept, a belief, a teacher that helps you build up strength and confidence. This is a beautiful part of the journey. Don't linger so long in these concepts, beliefs, or teachers that you stop searching, asking questions, or growing; this shifts you from a flowing river to a stagnant pond. If anything, become a flowing river and cascade as a waterfall below, and share your wisdom with others.

Teaching helps create a solid neural pathway where you can turn the lessons into your habits. Linger here for a bit, and let a vibrant pool of knowledge be shared in your community. In time, struggle will erode a solidified belief in the form of a challenge and break ground for you to continue to flow.

BARRICADE OR COMMIT

Refusing to meet struggle builds a barricade and blocks your path—mentally, physically, spiritually. You have a choice. We all have the choice. Build a barricade or commit to the path.

Committing to the path requires a deep faith in yourself and in something higher. This is where many feel abandoned in their growth. Afraid to trust themselves because of past failures and transgressions. Unable to believe there is anything bigger than themselves because of their repeated suffering.

For the faithful and the faithless, belief remains an unspoken struggle that can barricade your path. Removing the boulder seems too laborious. This is where two paths in the road diverge—and we choose the one that promises the greatest reward and the least amount of faith.

Chapter 17

THE "LET IN"

"We get to choose who we let in to our weird little worlds."

—ROBIN WILLIAMS

. . .

"You know what truly aches?
Having so much inside of you and not having
the slightest clue of how to pour it out."

—KAREN QUAN

BE CAREFUL WITH WHAT YOU LET IN. I DIDN'T FULLY UNDERSTAND that lesson until my house was full of strangers. The thoughts and beliefs of others disguised as my own were hidden in plain sight. Now that you have emerged on the other side of the tunnel and you have learned to shine your own light to illuminate your path, it might be time to go through your house and purge some old boxes of beliefs, feelings, and projections that you have held on to for far too long. It may also be time to upgrade your "security system" (mindset) and evict some squatters that are inhabiting crucial space for your growth.

YIN/YANG

Not just a Disney *Frozen* musical number, letting go is a recurring theme in most wellness coaching. The simplicity of its power overshadows the complexity of its teachings. If letting go was as straightforward as someone taking out the trash, then perhaps it would be less difficult. However, the emotional and mental residue is sticky and clings to us. This makes the act of letting go messy, uncomfortable, and honestly, stink to high heaven. What will it take to fully let go? *The answer is to first examine what you let in.* There are many individuals who will say that they don't hang around negative people and that they don't even allow negative people into their lives. No one can completely shield themselves from negativity. You could shut yourself into your home, never watch the news, delete all of your social media accounts, and turn off service to your cell phone. It still wouldn't be enough. The negative space, even if it is merely the absence of thoughts within your mind, is a part of the duality of struggle.

Struggle is not exclusively negative, but it most certainly isn't all positive either. Eliminating struggle, negativity, darkness, and so on is not the solution. Negativity is not the enemy, and positivity isn't the only answer. Harmony exists within both.

To better explain this duality of struggle, I want to share the lesson of yin and yang. Yin and yang is a concept of dualism describing how seemingly opposite or contrary forces may actually be complementary, interconnected, and interdependent. Their elements come in pairs—such as dark and light, cold and hot, male and female, north and south, passive and active, and so on—but note that the pairs are not static or mutually exclusive. While these elements appear to exist as opposing forces in nature, they can rely on one another to exist. Yin and yang lies in the interplay of these two components. Therefore, if we examine the struggle of letting go, we must also look at what we let in. This brings me to a word that few let in, as it is often labeled as inclusive to only a select few—faith.

FAITH DILEMMA

There might not be a word I had more experience with growing up than faith. In the time following my father's death, my mother took me to church. She went, as I imagined, for answers from God. I went to make puppets out of the collection envelope and sit quietly enough to go to Sunday school for the morning snacks. We have already learned that food is how I coped with my emotions (chapter 12). Even in the Sunday school classes where we colored pictures of Jesus and made unnecessary amounts of macaroni crafts, faith was still the cornerstone of the teachings. It may have been the carb-induced food coma that distorted my understanding of faith, but it basically boiled down to a few simple concepts. Faith requires that you believe in something higher than yourself, that you are obedient, and that you are good for goodness' sake. Hold up. That last one is definitely a lyric from the popular Christmas song *Santa Claus Is Coming to Town*.

While the last concept seems childish and misinterpreted, I used to read the lessons as a youth leader and Bible study teacher that paint faith as parallel to behaving for Santa in order to get what you want for Christmas. (I warned you that you weren't going to like everything I said. Try to stay with me for a little longer, and I might bring you back.) Faith was a matter of obedience and trust. If I questioned my faith, then I was disobedient to God's teachings and, therefore, less of a true believer, or so I thought. I feared questioning the feelings that stirred inside of me, wanting to unravel the root of these teachings. Some of the early spiritual teachers I encountered would have me believe that any questions around faith were signs of a failed belief in God.

I wish that someone at church would have knelt down and reached out a hand to say to me, "What are your questions, child? Where does this fear stem from?" Instead, I was met with a more parental "because I said so," when I brought up any uncertainty in the teachings I was given—at least in church. My mother was not one to stunt my curiosity or thwart my interest in larger than life concepts. She did, however, offer me her favorite Bible verse to repeat as I investigated. Matthew 17:20, "If you have faith the size of a mustard seed, and you will tell this mountain, 'Move from here to there,' and it will move. Nothing will be impossible for you." At first, I thought she was saying the exact same thing the church was telling me. I just didn't have enough faith to move the mountains of my mind yet, but in time I would grow into bigger faith and mountains would move.

This Bible verse, which I printed and plastered on my dorm room walls, the desktop of my computer, and all over notebooks like some lovesick teenager, wouldn't make sense to me until I found myself at the edge of the ocean battling yet another period of depression (chapter 7). I never told you what drew me back from those icy shores. It was that Bible verse. The one that I can recall hearing for more than twenty years from my mother. The one that at times felt like another dismissal of my curiosity around faith. As I came to learn it that day, standing at the edge of my mental health, the verse meant that unshakeable trust and confidence within transform struggle from the mountain obstacle to the mountain of power from which I can stand. Faith moves through me and, as a result, is the mover of my obstacles.

I wanted to shout this understanding to the world from the mountain I had just ascended. As I drew in my breath to call out to everyone around me, above and below, a wind gust caught my words and gravity threw them to the ground while letting a clamor of thunder shake the earth to ensure no one could hear me.

REMOVE THE LABEL

Why was faith being silenced? I paused and realized that, when it came to faith, the label affixed to the Nalgene bottle of others was tainted with biases, religious doctrine, and exclusivity. It didn't carry the power of trust and confidence in the way I was experiencing. It was weighted by the agendas of man. I want to clear the air and make a new label for faith and let it shine for the power it holds—*it is the unshakeable confidence and trust in someone or something higher*.

I also believe that this gift is given to me from God. *But to be clear, I do not push anyone else to come to the same conclusion. If faith is to truly transcend its religious label, it must be free to instill unshakeable confidence and trust in one by their own terms and means.* My intention for sharing my faith is not to preach at anyone, but to awaken the possibility that through the understanding of faith exists a path to our highest self. Here we can eclipse the boundaries of time and space. Faith unlocks the attic (subconscious) that has been padlocked for so long. It opens the door to the true understanding that our struggle contains our power.

There are no religious prerequisites for its truth or power. It has been within you all along. This is why I asked you to examine what you have let into your house. The intruders and judgements, shame and guilt, fear and uncertainty are masking the faith that sits in the attic. The cobwebs and dust have created an unwelcoming space hindering your desire to explore it. The dust of your "external experiences" from your Eastern point has dampened your "spiritual" southern point.

Recall that your true self lies opposite of the southern point. The duality of north and south makes faith key in unlocking our true self. Yet religious believers and secular explorers alike have become blind to the teachings of faith as it relates to purpose and personal transcendence. When you hear something enough, it is easy to let its meaning get watered down or lose the mysticism it once carried. The compass that guides each of us is rattled by this missing puzzle piece.

Confidence and unyielding trust in ourselves is something many of us lack. This loss of trust has led many of us to look outside of our experiences (East), wisdom (West), and true self (North) in hopes that some other anchoring belief system (South) will appeal to our desire to be free of struggle. As much faith as I have had in my life, and as much belief as I have had in God, I have still faltered in my own confidence. I found that my relationship with God was cheated in blind faith. By the time I chose to be baptized, in college, I had slipped back into a childish vision of youth and believed that, in exchange for faith in something higher, God for me, I must relinquish confidence in myself. This is not the God I have come to know. And it took a great deal of time and surrounding myself with new spiritual teachers to realize that this was not what God wanted me to surrender when I gave my life to Christ.

Your spirituality compass point is your deepest belief system, and that must begin with belief in yourself. Otherwise, regardless who or what you give your trust and confidence to, you will give it blindly and compromise your authentic self. By standing in an unwavering confidence and trust in myself, I include my choices, my thoughts, and my actions. This is not taking away from God because giving my life to His service also comes from this same act of faith.

PERSONAL INVENTORY

In order to offer you a lesson in personal faith, I ask you to take pause, to take inventory. Return to your deepest belief system and ask yourself if this system came from a place of trust and confidence in yourself or from the experiences of other people's projected confidence for you. You may find that you are following programs, engaged in relationships, or involved in experiences that are causing you to struggle because they stem from offering up your confidence in someone else.

If you waiver in trusting yourself because past choices have led you down a deep and dark path of struggle, remember the wisdom in duality. Even the worst of struggle is not inherently all bad. Vacillating trust reveals that, by recognizing it, you have also created a sense of trust. I know how difficult that may sound. Sit with it as long as you need, but then return to the potential this "knowing" offers—we possess the question and the answer.

Answers beget more questions, and questions beget more answers. The circular pattern is a symbol of wholeness and the infinite. Faith extends our capacity to experience both: wholeness and the infinite.

YOUR TRUE SELF

You can change the language and rename faith to fit your true self. You are the guru, after all. These are your teachings to share. But maybe think about reclaiming what faith means in this world, and let its power ripple out like a drop in the ocean, magnifying with each person it reaches. With your wisdom and perspective, a language is added to the translation of other people's struggle and power in faith.

If you want unshakeable confidence and unwavering trust restored within you, take back your faith. Share your faith. Show others that the word isn't to be feared or confined by a label. Rip that label off, just like you stripped off the labels robbing you of your power.

Faith transforms you. Faith in action becomes your beliefs. And your beliefs become the driving source of purpose. Fear will try to keep you bound to the suffering of the struggle. But faith will restore the mastery in its teachings.

Chapter 18

THE WHITE RABBIT
OF STRUGGLE

"I'm late! I'm late! For a very important date!
No time to say 'Hello,' goodbye! I'm late. I'm late! I'm late!"

—WHITE RABBIT, ALICE IN WONDERLAND

THE WHITE RABBIT IN *ALICE AND WONDERLAND* ARGUABLY REVEALS one of the greatest barriers in our mastery of struggle—time. Time has a particularly emotional trigger for most of us that paralyzes our ability to step into action. I hope that this reality is a relief to anyone who reads this book. You are not the only person who feels like time is in cahoots with the universe, preventing your personal transformation.

When I examined my personal triggers, with time I realized they were entangled in the stories I told myself about struggle. The ideas that I read on mindset or activities freeing me of struggle were elusive. In the depth of struggle we seek guidance. We see and hear what we want to protect the vulnerable being within that is hanging by a thread. Time is just as much a part of the struggle as it will be the solution. The challenge lies in the time percentage spent in each (struggle & solution).

I wanted to believe that if I struggled with depression for three years, the solution should take far less long than the struggle. It's the solution, after all, so why would it take as long as the problem? That doesn't make logical sense. Or does it? I have worked with athletes that want to lose twenty years of weight in three months and get frustrated when it doesn't happen. As I see it, this develops because we are in such pain in the struggle that we just want it to end. It is easier to jump from program to program and see quick results for a moment than it is to see tiny shifts over a sustained commitment to the true solution.

"I don't want to see this body one more day in the mirror; I want it gone now!" But it took twenty years of yo-yo dieting, emotional eating, and depression to lead my body to this moment. I don't like admitting that, but if I cannot be honest with what brought me here, then what makes me think that I can be honest with what will get me out of it either? Time is a precious gift, and most days I have squandered it with doubts, fears, and unnecessary worry. Time, patience, struggle—they are the trinity of health.

Patience gives space for us to step back and fully see the struggle and the direction it has been trying to guide us in. Time is the permission to slow down or speed up in accordance with the level of effort that is necessary to fully master the struggle or struggles we are experiencing. I mention both slowing down and speeding up because not everything requires us to linger. Sometimes we have to pull off the band-aid and expose the wound to air to get some healing. You also can't pick at the scab as it begins the healing process.

How do you apply this process? Begin with how you speak of time. The way you tell others about your time will reveal key insights into what struggle time really represents. If you say, "I never have time," perhaps what you are really saying is, I am trying to keep myself busy enough so that I don't feel the pain of _____. Fill in what that might be. Maybe you are staying busy and losing time because your relationship is falling apart and you aren't ready to face it? Maybe you are lacking time because sitting with your thoughts for too long leads you down the rabbit hole of all the ways you are "not enough"? Or maybe you are running out of time because it is easier to hide behind time than it is to admit that you aren't ready to take the actions necessary to make real change. These are all hypotheticals, but I have witnessed each firsthand.

THE GIFT OF TIME

I have convinced myself that there aren't enough hours to be better in my business, but I found time to watch a movie. I have told myself that I'm too busy to see friends and that's why I never go out, but the truth is that I have so much anxiety over going out that I hide behind time's wall of excuses.

Time, like struggle, requires your complete honesty. If you try to convince time that you need more of it, beware. You will get more time, but not always in the way you hoped. You will get more time in your current struggles. Time doesn't hear you say, I need more time to get my life in order. It hears, I need the push from you to make me see that I need to make my life a priority now! Time doesn't hear, I need to lose 10 pounds for my wedding. It hears, I need to address why I am always at odds with myself. So it gives you the gift you never wanted in struggle: more time with struggle.

You might think of the gift of time as something that means more minutes doing what you love. Time gives us what we need, not always what we want. That is real love. Time knows that healing and transformation are not fads or quick fixes. They require patience and deep faith in yourself. The minutes, hours, days, and years are gifts of permission to fail, to fall down, and to know that with time you can get back up. Time is not a punishment. When it runs out on a job, relationship, or modality for coping with mental health, it isn't the end. It is the end of that chapter and the beginning of a new one.

IN YOUR TIME

Struggle Guru, I need to remind you that your path is uniquely your own. This truth is equally empowering as it is frustrating. When you see someone in a similar struggle seemingly "snap out of it," you default to comparison. You look outside of yourself for guidance with the purest intention of changing as well. The eastern experiences (eastern compass point) give rise to our wisdom (western compass point), but without roots in our spirituality (southern compass point), your true north will be askew.

Your purpose and legacy are not running away from you, but time realizes that there is still more to learn before you are ready. This might be the lesson I have disliked the most. Truly believing that time was on my side and that in MY time I would achieve various levels of transcendence in my versions of highest self is a daily practice. Some days I believe it more than others. Some days, I stand at the ocean's edge in tears crying out for mercy to make the pain stop. Other days, I am standing in the valley letting the echoes of triumph permeate the foothills around me.

Time isn't my enemy, but I am still working on us becoming friends. This relationship requires trust, honesty, and vulnerability. I had to open up about the storyline I told myself about my time struggle as well as the ways in which those stories became my biology. Struggles are the stories we share, the beliefs that we engrain in the grooves of our minds and that become the actions we take as a result. As you work through your mastery of struggle, slide into the grooves of your storyline around time. If time is etched firmly in a space of negativity and you have built a barrier rather than harnessed its path, take a moment to pause.

TIME MANAGEMENT FALLACY

Many of us arrive to the conclusion in our pause that time is, in fact, a barrier in our lives. We deduce that the solution is time management. If we are better at how we manage our time, we will also become better equipped to manage struggle. This fallacy can lead to even more struggle. I have sat across the table from coaches who tell me to fill my planner with as much activity as possible and to leave room listed as "free space." The time block is a strategically created space for me to "do as I please." It was even referred to as a "buffer space" that would help manage my stress if another activity or event I had in my planner bled over into another activity. This "buffer space" was meant to keep me in line.

It didn't work. I found that I was becoming less capable of knowing just how long certain meetings, activities, and events would take, which meant that the "free space" was always getting erased. I learned that I had no concept of boundaries, value, or what I really needed.

Let me give you an example. I would set up a one-on-one

meeting with a potential client (athlete) and allot 45 minutes. At the meeting, I would get stopped by others I knew at the coffee shop I met, or my athlete would share some amazing story that would inevitably sidetrack the conversation, and suddenly, it would be two hours later. While I appreciated the time we had and was still on track, so to speak, because of my "free space" block, I was even more anxious and drained after spending more time physically, mentally, and emotionally than I anticipated. I might have time on my side, but my body and mind were not ready to endure an even longer day. I shifted time around but forgot that energy would also be displaced by this extension of interaction.

Disclaimer: The section that I am about to share is purely based on my personal observations. Feel free to question it and argue your own point of view.

FIRST LAW OF THERMODYNAMICS

The Law of Conservation of Energy states that energy can neither be created nor destroyed; energy can only be transferred or changed from one form to another. In my meeting example, if I spend an hour and fifteen minutes of mental focus more than I anticipated, that energy has to come from somewhere. I have found that it comes at the expense of my physical body. Now, if I was supposed to work out after the meeting, I would feel more drained than usual. I also used more mental focus than anticipated, which resulted in a serious drop in my motivation. After many similar scenarios, I couldn't help but wonder why I wasn't feeling more motivated or focused when I had managed my time appropriately and was still sticking to my schedule.

When I took pause with my time, it revealed my energy leak. I was not going to be motivated or consistent in my workouts when I planned them in the middle of the day. There was too great a chance that I would feel too depleted to give my best. That's when I committed to morning meditations and workouts. Before anyone could ask for my time, I would make time for myself. I would energize my body and mind to prime it for the daily workload. I noticed a huge shift in my ability to complete tasks and commit to my personal wellness.

Not everyone is a morning person. I am not suggesting that you get up early just because I do. I am pointing out that you need to take time to evaluate a few things: Where is your energy leaking? Is your time management actually creating a leak in your energy? Is time really the struggle? Or is the struggle how energy is transferred?

Don't rush this evaluation. Remember that time will only extend the struggle you have with it if you try to hastily brush past it. I encourage my students and athletes to keep a journal for a week of the activities they do and how their energy level felt at three points of the day: waking up, middle of the day (between 12 and 1 p.m.), and right before bed. After observing your energy patterns for a week, notice if there are "energy leaks" that may contribute to a dip in motivation or if you have specific "charge" moments that are helping you create habits of real change.

TIME OUT!

I hope that by this point in the book, guru, you see that struggle's storyline has the power to change you. If you want lasting change, then it includes changing your relationship with time. You might need to step back and unload some activities right now. You might even throw out a few more "Noes" to some people you love in order to see the full picture. It's time to go full Zach Morris from *Saved by the Bell*, and take a time-out and talk through the struggle(s). (If this metaphor is lost on you, please go to YouTube and find the reference.)

Give yourself permission to step back and see all the struggles, not just the ones that are most obvious. Sometimes the little cracks in the foundation that go unnoticed are what brings the entire house down. As a Struggle Guru, you have time on your side. Give it the space it warrants to help you master its lessons.

Chapter 19

ARE WE THERE YET?

"I've learned that fear limits you and your vision. It serves as blinders to what may be just a few steps down the road for you. The journey is valuable, but believing in your talents, your abilities, and your self-worth can empower you to walk down an even brighter path. Transforming fear into freedom—how great is that?"

—SOLEDAD O'BRIEN

IT'S TIME TO TAKE THE EXPERIENCES OF WHAT I HAVE SEEN AND studied on my path and transform that information into something powerful. Rather than getting "done" with things and saying, "Onward, onward, onward," I'm thinking, *Yes, onward, but I also have all this intel. It's time I use the experiences of my life and heart to shape the landscape of where I am going. You can do the same.*

Doing so requires us to look back at our struggles and ask ourselves where we could do a little more.

What was left in the tank over the last week? Month? Year?

Where could you have given more? Taken more of a chance?

What chances do you see that you didn't take? What struggle stood in your path?

The small patterns we replicate shape who we are, and if we continue down the path of struggle without heeding its speed limit or road signs, we might blow past the very path we needed to exit from the struggle to get to a more fulfilling destination.

So as you pause and think about the questions just posed, ask yourself, *Why?*

CLOUDS IN THE HEAD

As a coach and teacher, I found myself holding back. I was too afraid to believe I was capable or deserving of things, so I clouded my headspace with—busyness.

When I am busy, I can imagine I am useful. So I post videos of workouts, beach walks, retreats, and events. But when I finally sit with myself, I realize none of that makes me happy. *I am just masking the desires and goals I have with hurried thoughts and tasks that keep me distracted from the real struggle I need to face in order to fully experience joy in my life.*

Swept away by the wave of conformity and comparison, I have lost sight of what brings *ME* joy. And it isn't a busy life.

Most of us make endless lists and plans, and fill calendars and journals with activities because the devil resides in idle hands, *but where in all the planning and journeying did we forget to wrestle with struggle?*

You are, after all, a Struggle Guru; *where on your day planner did you add that in?* Have you ever just sat on the back porch sipping a glass of wine and thought, *Damn, that was fucking hard! But I got through it.*

And look at HOW you got through it. I'm not telling you that you have to psychoanalyze every struggle, but if putting a gold star on your refrigerator helps you feel like a Struggle Guru badass, go for it.

TRUE ADVENTURE

This is your invitation to join the *Struggle Guru adventure program*. Just like you attend seminars on new software or networking events to meet others in your field, the struggle program is your chance to expand your horizons. Don't worry, bags under the eyes and stray gray hairs are not included in this package.

I encourage you, though, to set aside time for the notion of Struggle adventures each quarter. By creating controlled events that push the boundaries of your struggle mastery, you are investing in your ability to map out alternate routes for the various mountains of struggle you might experience. Look at the answers to questions in this book you have written down. *What areas of your compass need to be filled in? How might you create a Struggle adventure that helps fill in some of the blanks?*

As you choose your adventure, it doesn't have to be a physical activity. Maybe art is outside your comfort zone, so you attend a four-week drawing workshop every Monday night. Maybe you are terrified of heights and you spend an entire weekend at a women-only climbing event. Or perhaps you are scared of animals and you attend a petting zoo. The program is really about facing fears. **Harness the power of your struggle to help you grow.** You don't have to love every moment of it—*but you might*.

MY PERSONAL STRUGGLE ADVENTURE

I have been a runner my entire life, but participating in an ultra-race seemed crazy to me. I pretended like I had no interest when someone would mention one, but secretly, I was terrified that I just wouldn't be able to complete one if I tried. *And how embarrassing would that be? For a lifelong runner to fail at something running-related would be mortifying, right?* But in 2019, I decided it was time. I was all in. I had never done a trail marathon, so I thought, *Let's go for fifty miles.*

Hahaha, I am still laughing at the absurdity of making that decision.

The training was nothing like I expected. Mostly because less than a month into the training program that my dear friend and running guru Valerie Hunt had written, I was nearly clipped by a car on an icy road and strained my perineal tendon in my foot and my flexor digitorum longus (my calf). I couldn't run a month into the training, so I took every run workout and made it a row workout. Then I decided to challenge my mental toughness by rowing a half marathon, full marathon, and 50 km (31.1 miles) on the erg (indoor rower).

Valerie immediately responded, "I have done many ultras and can tell you that I would never put myself mentally through a 50-km row." What I heard in those words was, *Kirsten, you are mentally ready for this race.*

I didn't want to stop there either. This was the tip of the proverbial training iceberg! I studied all the struggles. My inner guru wanted to know all the ways in which I might be able to see the struggle and work through it. (It was the surf scenario all over again; Chapter 7.) I observed what others ultra-runners said and did, and felt and lived, but I took it with a grain of salt. Or in the case of fifty miles, a whole *lot* of salt. I felt pain in parts of my body that have always been strong, and the parts that always hurt felt *amazing*. I experienced so many different types of struggle (some small), and in the end, as I finished, I was so in love with the struggle. Not the distance or the medal, but the struggle.

In that race, I realized I hadn't even scratched *the surface of* struggle. I had experienced so many different types of physical and mental struggle in my life that I had initially thought, *This must be the one I need to check off my list to really solidify my "guru status."* And yet, when I crossed the finish line, I just burst into laughter. The guy placing the medal around my neck was confused; my crew member probably thought I was delirious. But it wasn't that. I was laughing because *struggle had reminded me that it is everywhere. And that no amount of mileage, racing, or human suffering will stop it from continuing to show up—but I do have the option to get smarter through each struggle.*

TOUGH LOVE

When I vary the types of struggle I engage in, I also expand the circle of people who relate to this struggle. Try this out for yourself: If you want to complete your first Ironman, find someone who has completed one and spend time with them. Join training groups and soak in the knowledge. Or, if you are struggling with financial planning, seek out seminars and workshops at local business groups. The journey of struggle will only prolong if you are unwilling to get into the trenches.

As someone who struggles with anxiety over social gatherings, I find the hardest step is the first step out the door. When I arrive at workshops, trainings, or even meet-ups, I start to relax a little. Once the knowledge begins to flow, I feel at ease knowing that there are resources that exist to help me in my struggle. But I have to be willing to seek them out. So do you.

The "tough love" moment is that you must seek out the information. And not every resource will be helpful.

SERVING FROM THE SAUCER

Deciding not to engage in the "struggle process" at all only multiplies the struggle you feel. It may begin at home with sorting through your struggles and prioritizing what needs your attention first. Compiling the lists isn't enough. Your mind will try to protect itself and default to "busy." The to-do lists will pile up, and the number of times you say "yes" to others who need help will rise exponentially. You will feel drained, burned out, and even more stressed out.

I reflect on a conversation I heard with Maya Angelou. She was talking about how she is able to help others. She said, "I serve from my saucer, not my cup."

When you serve from your saucer, you are serving from a place of *overflow*. Serving from your cup depletes you, and when life takes all that it needs from you, there you stand with nothing. Tapping the cup in the hope one last drop will fall to your parched lips, you find—emptiness. Busy work is serving from the cup, not the saucer.

Struggle requires more overflow. I know it sounds absurd to seek out more struggle to fill your cup. It doesn't make sense that struggle can give you more energy, focus, and growth.

I am the first to protest such lies, but despite my great protest, the truth remains: Struggle has made me stronger, healthier, and smarter.

The untrained mind will act like a small child on a road trip. Repeatedly it asks, "Are we there yet?" Do not be lured into this trap: The journey ends when we take our last breath. As someone who has seen another person's final breath, I assure you that given the chance, no one in this situation would be in a rush to reach this moment.

If you can begin to release the pressure of having all the answers now, or "having it all together," you are opening yourself up to fully experiencing your life.

You don't have to prove to *anyone* that your life is meaningful.

There are no bonus points in the next life for having the biggest house, cutest family, and giving until you break. You were divinely created for a purpose that is uniquely your own. The more you compare, the more blind you become to the power bestowed upon you and only you.

It takes guts to embark on the journey. It takes heart to stay the course. It takes a true guru to know that the only thing you can master on the path is within.

Chapter 20

A THOUSAND-PETALED LOTUS

*"Whenever you should doubt your self-worth,
remember the lotus flower. Even though it plunges
to life from beneath the mud, it does not allow the dirt
that surrounds it to affect its growth or beauty."*

—SUZY KASSEM

WHILE "OM MANI PEDME HUM, OM MANI PEDME HUM" IS SOFTLY
chanted in class, the teacher invites us to try a mudra to help us
connect to the mantra being chanted.

The lotus mudra (symbolic gesture) involves keeping the
base of the hands together, along with the pinkie finger and
thumb. The index, middle, and ring fingers gently open, and
the shape of a lotus flower can be seen. The practice today is
themed around Thich Nhat Hanh's book, *No Mud, No Lotus*.

I think to myself, *Okay, okay, I can get into this. It's actually
pretty soothing.*

Then I squirm a little on my block because my spine is not used to being so upright, and my hips feel like they have been bound in chains for a thousand years. I open one eye to glimpse around the room to see if this chant and hand gesture was my secret initiation. But I see that everyone else is doing the same, and I close my eye again, still rather skeptical of what I am doing in this class. I can hear the teacher encourage students to chant along with her as the music volume rises. I concede and join in.

I start to unconsciously get louder in my chant as the instruments sweep me away in their rhythm.

Wait! What's that? Did the music stop? Was I the ONLY ONE still chanting? Damn it, I KNEW this would happen. It WAS my initiation.

I can feel my face turning fifty shades of red as the teacher instructs us to slowly open our eyes.

No, wait, I could just keep mine closed a little longer. Maybe people will forget that someone was still chanting. Is it too late to fake a coughing attack and slink out of the room and retreat to my car? I don't need my mat, I can buy another one. Actually, I won't buy another one. This is humiliating, and I am never coming back.

The internal dialogue seems to chatter for what feels like the full sixty-minute class, but it has only been a micro-moment. I open my eyes, and no one is staring at me. It would seem no one heard my outburst after the music stopped, or at least no one is letting on that they heard it.

I unclench my jaw and breathe. As I listen to Tracy, the teacher, share the story behind the lotus, it starts to resonate with exactly where I am struggling in my life right now.

She begins, "The lotus flower grows in the shallow and murky waters. They enjoy sunlight and warmth but are intolerant to the cold. This is why they are not seen blossoming in the winter. A sacred flower in Buddhist culture, the eight-petaled lotus symbolizes cosmic harmony. A thousand-petaled lotus represents spiritual illumination. A bud is where potential resides."

She goes on to quote from the book, "Just like the lotus, we too have the ability to rise from the mud and bloom out of the darkness and radiate into the world."

MUD

I purchase Thich Nhat Hanh's book almost immediately after taking the class. Its wisdom is still influencing the students I teach today.

No Mud, No Lotus addresses suffering and how we try to cover it up in consumption. People don't like to be with pain. Thich Nhat Hanh relates that many will try to seek a way to run away from it by consuming content, information, food, drugs, television. We will use anything we must to keep us from sitting face-to-face with suffering. The mud of suffering at times feels too great to witness. It's easier to stare at the blank sky than sift through the mud.

Yet... *the source of growth is in that mud*. You know it to be true, and when you make it through the mud and your lotus petals open up, you rejoice in it.

Quickly we share the wisdom of overcoming, and just as quickly we forget that we will continue to cycle through struggle and suffering throughout our lives.

If you can imagine yourself a lotus flower, you can see that you need the mud. Transformation occurs in this place.

Take that mud and plant in it the seed of potential. Let it bloom.

SOURCING

The crystal-clear waterfall that cascades down into the almost unexplainable blue water below is where many of us want to grow. It's beautiful there. Energy moves with the water, and the pools below feel like wells of wisdom collecting at the bottom. It's an image we have been sold, perfectly packaged, and it's neatly tied up with a bow. We love it!

No one tries to buy real estate near a swamp. They can't give away the mucky waterfront property. But the prices for the waterfall view or pristine oceanfront cost us *everything*. Sometimes more than we have. We put ourselves in debt for the dream we have been sold.

Each piece of land offers something different. The mud-filled water is free. It requires only your love and attention. Who has time for that? The waterfall and oceanfront have everything you ever wanted without the work. Or do they? When you evaluate what is being offered, consider the source. *Who stands to gain from this proposition? Where will you plant your lotus?*

We drink from the cups of many, but refuse to believe that the source of our thirst and ability to quench it reside within. *The reality that we contain both the answer and the question feels too philosophical, and it doesn't exactly solve the current struggle we are working through.*

Each time I land on my mat or hit the trails, I am confronted with the reality that more often I am the seed of potential than the flower of enlightenment. The relentless progress through the murkiness of life requires a resilience I am not sure I possess. When I gaze into the distance, I can see the crystal water and emerald green treetops in the distance. I wonder, *Why I am staying on this muddy path??*

I begin to seek out any way to bridge the gap from my

path to the pristine ecosystem of beauty I see just on the other side. From the very first glimpse I had of all the beautiful land around me, I shift my training, education, and desires to revolve around acquiring its wealth. But it seems like each time I seek out information about how to acquire this life, it costs me more and more of myself.

The crystal-cascading water won't accept me and my muddy seed of potential. I've uprooted my lotus flower and tried to transplant it into an environment that could not allow my seed of potential to grow and flourish. In fact, as soon as I begin to grow and others see the beauty of my petals, they tear one of my petals off or expose me to the cold, bitter realities of their environment. It is enough to send me into hibernation! And any time I dare to let my petals bloom, I am rolled back into a space of "potential," but never fully reach any enlightenment.

As I stay hidden in my shell, I wonder, *How many other people's lotus flowers are out there, just like me? How many others have been lured into the beauty of the "better life" and then find themselves forced back into a shell they have outgrown?*

It's cramped being forced back into something you are too big for. It's a lot like watching all 5'11" of me get out of a Smart car. I look like a giant coming out of a roller skate.

UNFOLDING

Slowly, slowly, I break free of the too small shell I've been forced into, and return to the mud—return to my teacher. I let the seasons help me blossom and bloom. I experience small flickers of enlightenment and try my best to retain its wisdom. I have even begun to see among the muddy waters the plush emerald moss, and the larger-than-life forest growing closer to the heavens.

It occurs to me that the waterfall is beautiful, but it is far more impressive when you hike up the mountain yourself, and rappel down it, soaking in its wisdom. But I am also aware that there are those who would always rather drive up to a parking lot, step outside their door, and see the beauty from behind a fence. They will snap their photo and brag to the world, but leave with no more wisdom or appreciation for what they saw.

I've become more conscious of where I am sourcing my wisdom. The practice in class with Tracy exploring the lotus flower is one I return to often as a way for me to tap into the questions and the answers I have within me.

If your consciousness is a well of knowledge, be careful from what wells you fill your cup. Some wells may look like waterfalls, flowing and life-giving. But they may cost you access to your well, and ultimately deplete you.

Never allow anyone to convince you that the only way to your power is to give them access to yours first. There are many amazing life-giving power-propelling bodies of water around you. You will recognize them by their lotus petals.

Struggle gurus carry the beauty and wisdom of the lotus and the courage of a lion. They aren't afraid to lead from the mud. Struggle gurus don't let the dark, deep, muddy water of their past be a blemish to their seed of potential. Instead, it nourishes the unfolding of yet another lotus petal.

The thousand-petaled lotus will take a lifetime of practice and struggle. It is said that at death, the fully realized yogi leaves consciously through the thousand-petaled lotus, without struggle; they are fully aware that it's their time to leave the world. Death is mastered and suffering ends. It reminds me that as long as I am struggling and still breathing, there is still more to be learned.

Breathe in your power, gurus.

Maybe no one has told you, or perhaps you needed reminding, but *you are powerful right now in this moment*. You aren't powerful because I said it or anyone else did, but because it's your truth. Infinite power exists within you. The frustration is that you might already know that, but haven't been able to tap into it.

Look around and make sure that your lotus seed is in a place where it can grow. That might mean uprooting from the crystal-clear body of water you have planted yourself and planting in the mud. You should know by now this book isn't going to tell you that it is easy, or that there are any shortcuts. The thousand-petaled lotus cannot emerge without the mud.

If you feel overwhelmed by the idea of such a change, start with small acts of struggle mastery. Start with the gift that each of us possesses—life. Place your hand on your heart and feel it beat beneath it. As long as you can still feel your heart beating, you have the capacity to master any struggle in your life. You *get to start again*. It's not a chance that everyone has, and those of us fortunate enough to still have this gift should honor it.

Your gift isn't amplified by your job title, the size of your pants, the speed of your marathon, the dollars in your bank account. **Your gift is amplified by sharing your story**. Stop letting others tell you that you are too young, too old, not pretty enough, or not smart enough to offer the world your gifts.

Invoke the courage of your inner lion that wastes no energy worrying what others might think of it. Instead, it follows its instincts and leads with confidence. Practice faith daily to build up your unshakeable confidence and trust in yourself again.

THE CALL

You can finish this book and still feel pain, be working through depression, or have low self-confidence. It doesn't mean the book has failed you. This book isn't the cure. It isn't the answer. It's the call.

If you have been waiting for a sign, here it is. What you do with it is entirely up to you.

I'm calling for you to unite. I have been searching for you. I need you. The world needs you. Unity creates powerful change. There are some struggles in this world that need eradicating, and you just might be the only person who has the answer.

Chapter 21

I FINISHED, NOW WHERE IS MY MEDAL?

"The most difficult thing is the decision to act, the rest is merely tenacity.
The fears are paper tigers. You can do anything you decide to do.
You can act to change and control your life;
and the procedure, the process is its own reward."

—AMELIA EARHART

THE SAND IS HOT AND KEEPS HER ON HER TOES. SHE RUSHES FORward for the volleyball, fully extending her body to save the play. It pops up, and her partner leaps into the air and slams the ball over the net with fierce power and force. The opponent's split-moment stutter in footsteps leads her to stumble and miss the point. Cheers fill the air with a buzz of excitement. *The USA Women's team wins!*

The female players on the American team rejoice and throw their arms around one another. They fist-pump to the stands and catch a flag tossed to them. The two run around the hot sand with the flag waving back and forth through the air with pride.

The announcer comes over the loudspeaker, "Thank you everyone for attending the Olympics; we will see you again in four years."

The referees leave, the media packs up, the stands start to empty. The two women look at one another and wonder where everyone is going.

"They haven't even given the medals yet?" one woman says.

"Oh, they don't do that anymore," a coach replies from the sidelines.

The champions slink down into their chairs, and their mood immediately changes. They look at each other with the same expression reading, *No medal? But we worked so hard. And we are the champions!*

Could you imagine making it all the way to the Olympics and winning and then… nothing? *That's it. You won. Congrats. Move on.*

How many people would still want to compete if this was how high-end competitions ended? And what if no one televised it, and no one wrote about it? What if no one even knew it was happening, and the only people who cared were those in the competition? Those involved in the competition would leave empty-handed at the end, with nothing to show for it. The reward is knowing that you did it. Let's not forget to add that you had to pay your way, and there is no financial reward for winning. Now, *how many of you would sign up for that?*

Very few, if any. Realistically, no one would sign up for that, but I know there are a few people who want to pretend like they would still be interested.

This is exactly what happens when you overcome struggle:

You do it, and nine times out of ten, it's not an athletic event or "major" achievement that people are invited to or in attendance to. *You* will be the only one who knows that you did it. No banners, no parades, and certainly no medals.

Struggle gets fewer and fewer sign-ups because people want to be *seen*. And since you have come this far in the book, you realize you don't need to fall prey to the "influencers" out there anymore. Screw that, you are ready to BE the influencer. *Right? Wrong.*

You didn't get all this way in the book to shrink back to some shallow idea of what it means to become the Struggle Guru. Speak to a Tibetan monk who has given up everything to offer a life of service. No possessions, no attachments. No rewards—not in this life anyway. The gurus you have read about in many of the eastern cultures are not in it for the glory and fame. They most certainly are not in it for the money. Gurus don't even call themselves "gurus." Others call them "gurus" because of the sage wisdom and experiences they offer.

You don't need a medal for your efforts. Your wisdom and experiences are felt in how you share and instruct others.

PART OF THE TRIBE

I believe that you are a Struggle Guru. From the core of my being, I believe in you.

Your power and potential is evident. I have seen many of you in classes, retreats, trainings. I have watched you pass me in the airport, at bus stops, and on crosswalks. You have bagged my groceries, built my house, taught me yoga, instructed me in biology. I have traveled the world and seen gurus aplenty. But they are masked behind a lifetime of labels. Buried beneath the anxiety, fear, and depression. Silenced by the power others exert over them.

You have a roar that could be heard across oceans and above mountains. You have truth and wisdom that can change not just *your* life, but the life of millions. Your reward is in the process.

When you first opened this book, you may have seen struggle as something to overcome and eliminate. If you still feel this way, it's time to read it again. Struggle is not an enemy of ours. Not for the gurus. It is our teacher.

"The past can hurt you. But the way I see it, you can either run from it or learn from it," said Rafiki. *Oh yes, I just quoted the Lion King. Ha ha. But it's true.* You can take the wisdom and continue to chase the highs, sit on your truth, and let the humble pie make you fat—or you can learn from it and let it give you power.

Struggle is not all rainbows and unicorns. It will club you like a caveman looking for a meal. It will burn like a raging forest fire at times. I'm not asking you to be the fake optimist in these moments. I am asking you to be strong. Fire is necessary in the forest to open the pine cones and let new seeds drop. The club might hurt, but you will learn how to maneuver and skillfully move. The journey never stops. The learning never ceases.

Don't be afraid of the master within you. Don't be too proud with it either. Struggle loves to humble us when we think we know too much.

I'm proud of you, Struggle Guru. It is an honor to have you in my tribe. This isn't the end. This is how our journey together begins.

Much love & gratitude Gurus,

GURU BEGINNINGS

*"If you are brave enough to say goodbye,
life will reward you with a new hello."*

—PAULO COEHLO

WELCOME TO YOUR SPACE, WHERE YOU WILL WORK THROUGH THE questions of this book and begin your journey as a Struggle Guru. You will find each chapter's questions outlined here for you to reference quickly, and there is space for you to write, draw, and scribble down any inspiration that arises in your practice. This is just the beginning of your journey. Let it be filled with exploration and wonder.

CHAPTER 1: MEET YOUR GURU

GURU PRACTICE

I remember my first visit with my guru. He had shown me that he could read my mind. So I looked at the grass and thought, 'My God, he's going to know all the things I don't want people to know.' I was really embarrassed. Then I looked up and he was looking directly at me with unconditional love.

—RAM DASS

American spiritual teacher Ram Dass speaks to a particularly eye-opening understanding of "guru" that has changed the way in which I understand its meaning. In the epigraph that starts this chapter, notice that he recalls meeting a guru who could read his thoughts, and he experiences shame and fear in this vulnerability. Dass is worried about what others will know, and how that will shape their view of him.

After sitting with this passage for some time, I realized that Dass could very much be speaking to his true self, or his divine inner guru—or that which some might call his consciousness. But let's explore what *you* think about it.

How does this quote change, in knowing this information? (Pause with that for a moment.)

_____

_____

_____

What if he is truly fearful of fully knowing himself, and his deepest thoughts and fears?

_____

_____

_____

To what reality will he be held accountable?

_____

_____

_____

What keeps you from showing yourself unconditional love?

_____

_____

_____

CHAPTER 2: FOLLOWING THE STARS

GURU PRACTICE

Spend some time with these questions and answer as honestly as you can. Remember each truth is here to help you master your struggles. With each practice of vulnerability you begin to transform your storyline and change your biology.

Are you living your story? Or is your story the watered-down version of someone else? Be honest with yourself.

What path are you on at this moment in your life? How did you get here? What education, experiences, and influences impacted this direction for you? Are you happy with where this path is leading, or is it time to change paths?

What are certain "givens" that you may have subconsciously believed you deserved in your life but have not received? Why do you think that you haven't received or achieved these "givens" yet?

CHAPTER 3: COM-PASS YOU ARE

GURU PRACTICE

FOUR POINTS OF YOUR COMPASS

Review the points on your directional compass. Afterwards, spend some time reflecting on your compass. Fill in the blank compass included or draw a completely new one with the information you discover while exploring these teachings.

Your **north** is set to experiences, education, and people that will help you solidify your true north, or your true self. (Dare I call your "north" your authentic self?) Here you want to spend the most time asking questions, challenging the "norms," and sitting with your thoughts.

Take your **southern** directional point. This is your spiritual influence. This point is impacted by your beliefs, understanding, and connections to consciousness bigger than yourself. It doesn't ask for a religious practice, but it does require you to evaluate your deepest belief systems. The roots of your beliefs will profoundly shape where your north points. Think about it: *North would have no value if there were no south*—just as the dark would be irrelevant if there were no such thing as light. Contrast deepens understanding. Take your deepest beliefs, and ask how these beliefs shape the person you want to be.

The **eastern** needle moves by the influence of external environments and experiences. This area of your compass will be tied to things outside of yourself. When you look at these external forces, you will find an internal footprint. Your access to education may have been limited, and therefore you see struggle in learning. When someone is deprived of the basic tools of education, how can we expect them to harness the internal power to overcome this? But we do. We ask students from lower-income cities and suburbs with no access to books or healthy learning environments to rise up. Therefore, some students internalize that they are uneducated or unteachable as a result of this experience.

The external environments and experiences of the east play a part in leading your **western** directional point, which is where we harness true wisdom. *Wisdom emerges from experience.* Not all wisdom is good. If the eastern point of your compass is broken by pain and suffering, your wisdom can reflect deeper bitterness and cynicism. The internal footprint becomes a permanent tattoo that cannot be scrubbed off. A cycle of struggle with no hope of changing direction becomes the new normal.

QUESTIONS TO ASK WHEN CREATING YOUR COMPASS

Evaluating your compass: "If it feels like your compass is shattered, and you haven't found the right teachers to help you reset it, *this* is your opportunity. You cannot take back the past. You can't right the past wrongs of inequality that you have experienced, or the distorted beliefs you have passively observed. You will have to get your compass out and take a look at it: *Where does it need mending? Where does it need my attention?*" (pg 29)

JOURNAL EXERCISE TO FOCUS ON EACH POINT OF YOUR COMPASS

What is one thing I have learned from external experiences this week? What is a piece of wisdom I have gained? How have my beliefs deepened? And what is one way in which I feel closer to who I want to be?

CHAPTER 4: UNIQUELY UNQUALIFIED

GURU PRACTICE

Spend some time reviewing these questions. After thinking about them, go for a walk or sit in quiet meditation. When you return this page, write down what thoughts bubbled to the surface. Do not edit or sensor your thoughts. Let them flow on the page in any form they come.

In what ways have you felt unqualified in your own life? (work, relationship, health, fitness, nutrition)

_____

_____

_____

_____

How has feeling unqualified impacted the choices you make in this area of your life?

_____

_____

_____

_____

Write down the areas in which you feel unqualified in the order of importance to you below.

_____

_____

_____

What are three fears you have in mastering this area of your life?

_____

_____

_____

What are three actions you can take immediately to address the first area you listed above?

_____

_____

_____

Write down a quote or mantra below that resonates with you and your ability to feel strong in who you are. Feel free to write this quote in multiple places where you will see it throughout the day.

_____

_____

_____

CHAPTER 5: A BAD CASE OF AUTHENTICITY
GURU PRACTICE

In what area(s) of your life do you feel like you are inauthentic? Write down small interactions, expressions that may make you feel inauthentic as well as glaring ways in which you are muting your voice.

What is your greatest fear when it comes to being completely authentic with who you are? Who are you most afraid to show the authentic you? (boss, friends, family, yourself)

What is one action step you can take today to bring you closer to your authentic self?

CHAPTER 6: THE POWER OF BEING SEEN

GURU PRACTICE

Being seen has many meanings. Take the next 2–5 minutes and write down what it means for you personally.

Review the passage from chapter 6 below. Then answer this question: How can I let others be seen? In what ways could I show someone that I really see them?

> "I see you, because I also see me." It's not oneness; it's wholeness. It's not individuality; it's unity. I want to be seen beyond the flesh, beyond my acts of kindness or service, beyond my clothing choices or life partner. I want the energy of a higher vibration within me to be felt and move in such a way that it also allows me to feel the vibration of every living thing on this earth.

CHAPTER 7: OCEAN TIDES

GURU PRACTICE

Re-read the passage from Ocean Tides below.

> "Much of my anxiety is rooted in thoughts that rip me
> out of the present. The thoughts are shortcomings of
> my past and fears of the future. As I studied what it
> means to be human, I had this awakening..."

> Each of us are human beings—a universally undeniable fact.
> "Am" is the first person present singular of the verb "to be"—a
> single person speaking about themselves in the present. One
> might conclude that we are designed to be fully present from
> creation. If we are human beings, then our divine connection is
> in *the now*." (pg 63)

After you read this passage again, what feelings immediately
arise? Does anything specific stand out to you?

_____

_____

_____

_____

_____

Make a list of your biggest fears. How many of these are the result of thoughts tied to your past or future? What part of that fear is present today? How can you address the feelings and emotions happening in this moment?

CHAPTER 8: THE NALGENE DILEMMA

GURU PRACTICE

EXPLORATION OF LABELS

"I am _____." Make a list of every label you have attached to the previous statement. After you have written them down, place a (+) next to the labels that make you feel positive and (-) next to the labels that feel negative. You might find that some labels leave you feeling fairly neutral. Place a (0) next to any label that has you feeling neutral. After you have made your list, close this book or the journal you wrote it in. Return to this page in a few days or a full week.

BACK TO THE PRACTICE

Now that you are back, look at your list of neutral labels. This is where we are going to start. Re-read the labels and see if you still feel completely neutral about each label. If any have changed, add them to your positive or negative list. Go by your heart, not your head. Your head will rationalize, categorize, and organize the neutral labels for you. Listen to what your heart says about each one.

_____

_____

_____

_____

After you have completed this, look at your list. If you still have neutral labels left, it's time to let them go. If they do not move you to happiness or move you to change out of sadness or anger, they are not contributing to your growth. They are leaving your mindset in neutral, which doesn't bring you any closer to mastery in struggle. I like to write labels down on a dry erase board and erase each one. Some write them on paper and shred, crumple, or burn them. It's up to you.

NEGATIVE LABELS

Examining the labels that make us feel "less than" are important in our mastery of struggle. Letting go of these labels will not be as simple as erasing them off a board or throwing them away like you did with your neutral labels.

Instead, I want you to search for the source of this label's origination. Examine no more than two or three labels. If the list is short, zero in on just one. Think back to the first time you heard that label. Maybe it was the first time you gave yourself the label. *What was the scenario? Who was there? How old were you?* Try to find as many details as you can. Now think of the most recent time someone labeled you this. *Or the last time you labeled yourself this? What similarities about the environment, people, or experience led up to this label?* Now for the big question, *"Can you alter any of these factors to reduce your exposure to this label?"*

Be vulnerable and honest with this answer. It's easy to respond with a defensive, "No, I cannot change any of these factors." You are in control of your side of the street in this story. There are factors you can influence. They may be factors that you are uncomfortable changing or fear tied to past decisions or future scenarios trying to thwart your change. Don't rush your thoughts. Remember it must happen in your own time.

POSITIVE LABELS

I have not forgotten about the positive labels. While it would be easy to just leave them affixed to your Nalgene bottle, they can still be very telling of the choices you are making in your life. What would you say are your top three positive labels? E.g. mom, entrepreneur, friend. Don't overthink your top three. Remember to listen to your heart.

Have these top three positive labels ever held you back from going after a goal or dream? Have you ever thought, I want to go back to school and become a nurse, but then stopped your internal action plan with a wall built around being a mom? Or have you considered taking a new volunteer position that would be incredibly fulfilling, but hesitated because it meant giving up time with friends? Even positive labels can alter the way we make choices.

For this practice, rather than thinking of any label you have given yourself or felt someone else gave you, I want you to write out what you want your life to look like in the next three months. Start small. What do you want your energy to feel like? What do you want your career to look like? How do you want your body to move? Who do you want to spend time with? Get as detailed as possible without adding labels. This will get tricky. Let me give you an example.

> **Labeled example:** I want to search for a new job in human resources that is in better line with my goals and values.

> **"Un-labeled" example:** I want to expand the types of opportunities I seek out to include professional positions that offer me a work-life balance and a strong sense of community engagement.

The first example specifically labels "human resources" and narrows your search based on a label. I can't tell you how many times I have helped students of mine find careers by searching their interests and skills over the job title. There are careers they didn't even realize they were qualified for or that existed to begin with, because they were so caught up in the label.

By expanding your dialogue into the emotional and neural pathways, you start coding a new language. This new language increases the resources to draw from as we work through struggle.

This will be a continuous practice. It gets to the core of what you really want and lets your authentic voice be heard. This is how you shake the way you think.

CHAPTER 9: ARCHITECTURAL GENES

GURU PRACTICE

EXAMINE YOUR FOUNDATION

Write down every "genetic trait" that you have used as an excuse (yes, an excuse) for why you are not where you want to be today. Now let's get real. Is this really the barrier? Or have you been creating cracks in your own foundation?

What type of house do you want to build? Examine the genetic factors that have felt like limitations and look at what resources you need in order to make them building materials for your house. Talk to others with similar genetic factors or experiences to help you make a "materials" list. Attend seminars. Seek out a coach. Find meetups. You are the architect of your life. What will you build?

If you want to get creative, you might even draw a house and fill it with the words and materials you need to build your house. Use the space below to get creative. Write, draw, sketch a blueprint.

CHAPTER 10: UNDER THE INFLUENCE

GURU PRACTICE

For your practice, return to the Leadership Markers listed in chapter 10.

Consistently rank the markers in order from qualities you possess most to least. After ranking your leadership markers, evaluate some ways in which you could work on the qualities you ranked the lowest. Struggle Gurus are leaders, and this practice helps you use your voice to connect with other gurus.

LEADERSHIP MARKERS

When you find someone whose influence has true power, you will see certain commonalities.

True leaders with influence give when they don't have to. They don't post about every donation or every hour they volunteer.

They care for others. Not because it helps them gain power, but because they are driven to leave the world a better place than they found it.

They grow continuously. Driven to never stop learning, these leaders love to challenge the way they think.

They live authentically. They don't speak love and compassion on the yoga mat, and then cut you off or tear down the cashier when the line is long. Who they are is transparent. They are not without flaw, but they don't try to hide the imperfection. They shine a light on the ways in which they are human.

They empower others. They are not fearful that sharing their knowledge or truth will rob them of their place in this world or the success they will achieve. Elevating those around them is just as much a part of their journey as the leadership they have acquired.

They manage hardship. They have bad days and feel overwhelmed like the rest of us. But they let hardship create opportunity for growth. They don't linger in the darkness when offered a light.

They serve with humility. They are humbled at the possibility that serving others has such a powerful reach. But they also recognize that this power exists within every human being; it's just untapped potential in some.

CHAPTER 11: SWIPE RIGHT, DODGE LEFT, STUCK CENTER

GURU PRACTICE

LISTING YOUR "TOP 5"

"Take a long, hard look at who you surround yourself with most consistently—the top five people with whom you spend the most time. If you don't like the people who appear in your "top five," you might want to reshuffle the deck: *You begin to emulate the people with whom you surround yourself the most.*" (pg 87)

For your practice, examine the top 5 people you spend the most time with regularly.

Do you like this list? Are they people who challenge you, bring you joy, and help you grow? No? Time to reshuffle. Sometimes we spend time with amazing people, but they are not the best influence for our growth. We might need to move them to number six and move someone new up. Truth is, some of your top 5 might be people you need to seek. Go back to your three-month goal list and see if you need to start seeking some new connections for your top 5.

CHAPTER 12: HUMBLE PIE IS MAKING ME FAT

GURU PRACTICE

In chapter 12, we discussed carrying the weight of other people's words and actions towards us on our shoulders. For your guru practice, revisit the questions at the end of the chapter. You may re-read the chapter before going into this practice.

In what ways has your voice felt silenced? Is there a way in which you can release the weight of other people's influence and pressure, and free yourself to fully "BE"?

_____

_____

_____

_____

_____

CHAPTER 13: RUNNER'S HIGH

GURU PRACTICE

LESSON PLANS

In chapter 13, you examined the many ways we mask struggle. It's time to pull back the mask and look at your biggest struggles. Write them down, give them a name. Draw them as a crazy monster. Say their names out loud.

_____

_____

_____

_____

Student Practice: Take the list of struggles you composed and pick one (most likely your biggest struggle). Write down every question that comes to mind about this struggle. What does it look like? What does it sound like? What human qualities does it possess? What obstacles has it created for you?

_____

_____

_____

_____

Teacher Practice: Imagine yourself as your teacher now. Write a lesson plan about the struggle your inner student selected. What information would you provide your student with to help them learn how to recognize it, navigate it, and mobilize through the potential obstacles? Find the answers to as many of your student's questions as possible.

_____

_____

_____

_____

Homework: Your assignment now is to take the questions and answers you have found and turn them into three action-able steps to help you master this struggle. Once you have your three action steps, select one. Work with this action step until you either notice the struggle easing, or it is becoming worse. Keep notes. Struggle Gurus always keep notes of their experiences because it might be the key for another Struggle Guru. Keep working through your action steps until you run out; then return to the practice of making a new list. Creating small lists of three is less intimidating and gives you space to let each action breathe. Do not rush the process. I know, that's not what you want to hear. Steady with your practice, guru.

_____

_____

_____

CHAPTER 14: PULL UP A CHAIR

GURU PRACTICE

"PULL UP A CHAIR"

Today, this moment, I am going to advise you to do something that makes you sit in discomfort. It doesn't mean you physically have to hold a pose, but *get outside your comfort zone, then sit with how this discomfort and uneasiness makes you feel.* Spend two to three minutes writing down everything about your experience.

CHAPTER 15: TUNNEL VISION

GURU PRACTICE

ILLUMINATE

Take a moment and reflect on the previous chapters: *Which chapter jumps out at you?* Don't overthink or analyze it. Go take that chapter and sit quietly, or find a place where you can walk and be with your thoughts. Run through the chapter in your mind and let the words, feelings, and experiences flow. If you are sitting quietly, you can set a timer for five minutes. If you are walking and want to walk for longer than that, you can; just place your phone on voice recorder and start talking it out. You can let the thoughts flow freely to help you work through this tunnel vision.

THROUGH THE TUNNEL MEDITATION

As you close your eyes, envision the chapter title you selected sitting at the end of the tunnel. Notice the length of the tunnel. Take in the shadows and light.

Are you the only one in the tunnel, or do you see anyone else? What thoughts or feelings arise as you think of the chapter you selected? How many different senses can you bring to this experience? Do you feel anything as you move through this tunnel? Are there particular surfaces you walk across?

Is there a breeze? What does the temperature feel like against your skin? Is there a familiar scent in the air as you walk? What subtle scents do you smell? Can you taste anything? What do you see?

Are there shapes, colors, people, things that you can make out as you walk closer to the end of the tunnel? As you move closer to the end, do you feel any differently than when you started?

Open your eyes.

Write down as much as you remember from this meditation. Don't worry about *how much* you remember; your mind is doing the heavy lifting by filtering out the pieces that are unnecessary.

NAVIGATING

Once you have completed the meditation exercise, it's time to make a plan. Look at your list and decide what action you can take based on this list. Divide your list into senses. Note which memories from your meditation correlate with sight, sound, smell, touch, and taste. This will help determine the means by which you can best navigate the tunnel you have chosen. (pg 114)

CHAPTER 16: PATH OR BARRICADE

GURU PRACTICE

In what areas of your life are you abandoning ship too early? (relationships, health, nutrition, fitness, professional life) What areas of your life are you sinking with your ship?

_____

_____

_____

_____

What tools would help you become a better captain of your ship? (This includes the wisdom to decipher between sailing through the storm and abandoning ship.)

_____

_____

_____

_____

CHAPTER 17: THE "LET IN"
GURU PRACTICE

DEFINE FAITH FROM YOUR PERSONAL PERSPECTIVE

What does unshakeable confidence and trust in yourself look like?

_____

_____

_____

_____

How will you know that you have it?

_____

_____

_____

_____

_____

CHAPTER 18: THE WHITE RABBIT OF STRUGGLE

GURU PRACTICE

Where is your energy leaking?

_____

_____

_____

_____

Is your time management actually creating a leak in your energy?

_____

_____

_____

Is time really the struggle? Or is the struggle how energy is transferred?

_____

_____

_____

CHAPTER 19: ARE WE THERE YET?

GURU PRACTICE

STRUGGLE ADVENTURE PROGRAM

"This is your invitation to join the *Struggle Guru adventure program*. Just like you attend seminars on new software or networking events to meet others in your field, the struggle program is your chance to expand your horizons. Don't worry, bags under the eyes and stray gray hairs are not included in this package.

I encourage you, though, to set aside time for the notion of struggle adventures each quarter. By creating controlled events that push the boundaries of your struggle mastery, you are investing in your ability to map out alternate routes for the various mountains of struggle you might experience. Look at the answers to questions in this book you have written down. *What areas of your compass need to be filled in? How might you create a Struggle adventure that helps fill in some of the blanks?*

As you choose your adventure, it doesn't have to be a physical activity. Maybe art is outside your comfort zone, so you attend a four-week drawing workshop every Monday night. Maybe you are terrified of heights, and you spend an entire weekend at a women-only climbing event. Or perhaps you are scared of animals, and you attend a petting zoo. The program is really about facing fears. **Harness the power of your struggle to help you grow.** You don't have to love every moment of it—*but you might.*" (pg 143)

Design a Struggle Adventure below that helps you push your boundaries as a Struggle Guru.

_____

_____

_____

_____

_____

_____

_____

_____

CHAPTER 20: A THOUSAND-PETALED LOTUS

GURU PRACTICE

What is your "Lotus Story?" Begin to write down the muddy experiences that have led you to find strength and beauty in your life.

_____

_____

_____

_____

_____

_____

_____

_____

_____

_____

Let this practice be a reminder that without mud, there would be no lotus flower. You cannot become a Struggle Guru without struggle. Let struggle be the mud that builds the guru within you.

CHAPTER 21: I HAVE FINISHED THE RACE, NOW WHERE IS MY MEDAL?

GURU PRACTICE

Sit somewhere quiet and see yourself standing on a podium in front a crowd of people receiving an award for Struggle Guru mastery.

How does that feel? Can you close your eyes again and, instead of envisioning yourself on a platform receiving a medal, imagine yourself in a place that brings you great happiness. The wind blows softly past you and whispers that you are a Struggle Guru. Congratulations on mastering _____ [insert struggle here]. I am so proud of you. What sensations do you feel in your body? Whose voice did you hear tell you those words? Feel the corners of your mouth lift as you smile. Take a few breaths in and out. Softly lift your eyelids.

Write down which visualization felt more rewarding and try to articulate why.

_____

_____

_____

_____

_____

Whose voice did you hear congratulate you? If it wasn't yours, why do you think it was that voice? Don't think too much about the whys. Let the heart once again guide your response. Then release the practice. Each time you return to this practice, write down anything different you see or feel. Over time, you will have a journal filled with collections of your mastery and wisdom from your inner guru.

REFERENCE

1   Sources of Human Psychological Differences: The Minnesota Study
    of Twins Reared Apart

2   Thomas J. Bouchard, Jr.; David T. Lykken; Matthew McGue;
    Nancy L. Segal; Auke Tellgen

3   Science, New Series, Vol. 250, No. 4978 (Oct. 12, 1990), 223-228.

ABOUT THE AUTHOR

KIRSTEN BEVERLEY-WATERS IS A MOTI-
vational speaker, author, movement coach,
and yoga teacher who leads workshops and
retreats around the globe. As the founder
of Aiiro Wellness, an online platform
and sharing space for health and healing,
she is an advocate for total wellness that
is centered around a deep mind and body connection. Kirsten
believes that vulnerable storytelling, strong laughter, and the
sweetness of a donut can cure almost anything.

www.aiirowellness.com